BRIEF
ENCOUNTERS
OF A
LEGAL KIND

BRIEF
ENCOUNTERS
OF A
LEGAL KIND

AUBREY ROSE

Lennard Publishing

First published in 1997 by
Lennard Publishing
a division of
Lennard Associates Ltd
Mackerye End, Harpenden
Herts AL5 5DR

A catalogue entry is available from the British Library.

ISBN 1 85291 134 4

Jacket design: Paul Cooper Design
Editor: Mark Stephenson
Production Editor: Chris Hawkes

Printed and bound in Great Britain by
Butler & Tanner, Frome and London

Contents

This book is dedicated to my wife Sheila,
who steadfastly deciphered and processed each
hand-written word, to my mother-in-law
Annette Glassman, who perused every syllable with
a keen and critical eye, and to my tax inspector,
who kindly suggested the title we have adopted.

Foreword

Lawyers and non lawyers alike will find this collection of 'Encounters' a source of enormous enjoyment. That is certainly true in my case. Once I started on the trail of Aubrey Rose's account of his experiences during 40 years of practice I could not stop until I came to the end. His stories are irresistible, amusing and humane. Easy to read they reveal a deep understanding of human nature.

I know Aubrey because his wife, Sheila, who I learn from this book was his first client, is my third cousin. Alas the world being what it is we have not seen anything like as much as we would have wished of each other over the years. I knew from others of his excellent work in seeking to promote better communal relations but I had little idea of the exotic nature and scale of his practice which the 'Encounters' reveal. This is despite the fact that I had cause to be grateful as a young barrister for being instructed from time to time by his estimable and then only employee Joffre Cumming-Bart who was one of the most charming of men.

It is a remarkable story which Aubrey has to tell. Sadly I doubt if a youngster entering the profession today can hope for a similar career. Starting at the grass roots without going to University, he established his own practice with a minimum of resources and then went on to become the champion, the adviser and confidant of those in need of help from all walks of life and from many parts of the globe. I find it difficult to believe that any other solicitor could have been involved in quite such a multi-coloured spectrum of work.

For reasons at which he does not even hint, Aubrey is approached out of the blue by a remarkable collection of clients. Mothers in distress, High Commissioners, kidnappers, Governments and entrepreneurs, they all sought his assistance which they got. His Jewishness did not deter his being approached by Muslims or Tamils. At the Brixton Inquiry conducted by Lord Scarman, he appeared alongside distinguished QCs He represented a shop lifter. He was at the centre of the campaign to establish a lottery. He was involved in complex libel actions. A commission was established to enquire into misdoing in Bangladesh and Aubrey became actively involved. A huge fraud was committed by a tax inspector and he was defended by Aubrey. This range of work in this age of specialisation is mind-boggling.

Reading this book, you are left with the strong impression that the explanation for his following is that Aubrey has deservedly acquired a special reputation. This irresistibly attracted to him those with problems of an unconventional nature. You suspect that for some clients he was approached as a last resort. For others he was approached because he was the only lawyer they felt could help them.

It is part of the attractiveness of this book that it brings you into contact with an extraordinary range of problems and different areas of litigation. In relation to this kaleidoscope of cases no one person could possibly be an expert and this Aubrey does not pretend to have been. For Aubrey and the reader each problem is a green field site. You are never bored. But obviously neither was Aubrey. He appears to have attacked the troubles of each new client with immense relish. The client received his total commitment, his well of sympathy and deep understanding for the human problem behind nearly every 'Encounter'. This and his obvious integrity and lack of personal motivation, I suspect, explain the reputation which has ensured his success.

In later years Aubrey had partners. They obviously had to tolerate a somewhat unconventional approach to work and fee-charging by Aubrey. Without this, it is likely we would have been deprived of the pleasure these 'Encounters' provide. I hope that this book will have the many other readers that it deserves and that they, like myself, will be grateful to his partners for their tolerance.

Lord Woolf of Barnes
Master of the Rolls

Chapter 1

Early Days

Introduction

As a youngster I had two ambitions: I wanted to be a writer and a lawyer. I have been writing all my life, whether published or not made no difference. Give me paper and pen and I was off, or at least the pen was off, as it seemed to have a mind of its own.

The lawyer part came from a practical bent in my family. A living had to be earned. I was also fascinated by this strange, but apparently influential, world. People in those days spoke in awe of solicitors, barristers, judges. My generation – the children of immigrants – sought status, influence, position. What I had heard about the law attracted me. 'Get him into an office', my mother was advised, 'best way to learn'. 'Don't bother about universities.' So an office it was.

My legal career began with my back to a blazing coal fire, high above Leadenhall Street in the City of London.

We had time in those days. I was an apprentice, a species known as articled clerk (now trainee solicitor). I reported to the managing clerk (now legal executive). I was apprenticed, or articled, to a solicitor (so far still a solicitor). In those far-off days of the late 1940s, that was how one entered the profession. Benjamin Disraeli and Charles Dickens both had a short session in it and went on to other things. David Lloyd George stayed the course.

Nearby in Cornhill, Charles Lamb once sat in East India House, pondering his *Essays*. A glance from my window indicated Whittington Avenue, where dwelt Dick and his cat. A few yards to the left had been the home of Rufus Isaacs, Lord Reading, former Lord Chief Justice. Not far away rose the great Tower of London, built by the Normans 900 years earlier for their protection. Also nearby were the Royal Mint, Lloyds of insurance fame, the Stock Exchange, the Baltic Exchange, the Royal Exchange, and the Bank of England. We were in the beating financial heart of the Empire, if not of the world. History surrounded us.

It was an old building in which we laboured, long since replaced by an anonymous, cost-effective giant with central heating, if not air-conditioning.

We had time indeed in those days. Sophisticated machinery – fax, word processors, computers – did not afflict us. Time recording was for factory workers. We stood with our backs to the fire, taking our time, talking, discussing. At lunch time (usually fairly extended) we sauntered over to Tower Hill and listened to the impassioned speakers on their platforms – political and religious, socialist and Soper – setting the world aright, watched cargo ships at anchor, barges chugging down the river. We worked hard, long hours. We did not rush. We learned our trade, not so much from books and lectures, but from what we did; from our cases, our clients, our prolonged discussions with our backs to the fire.

Many hours I spent in the Law Courts in the Strand. It rose like some bizarre château on the Loire, though erected only in the 1880s. I walked its corridors daily, miles of them, issuing writs, entering appearances, signing judgments, arranging executions (of inanimate objects only), appearing before lesser judges known as masters, whose chambers surrounded a frenetically busy area aptly called the Beargarden.

This palace of justice fascinated me. I spent much of my early life there, often sitting in court after court, admiring the dignity, the presence, and the prescience, of our judicial hierarchy. Some became my heroes. One, whose retirement should have come years before, was said to have lucid intervals.

Across the Strand, past the statues of former local resident Samuel Johnson, four-time prime minister William Gladstone, and Battle of Britain victor Air Marshal Lord Dowding (later moved and re-erected close to the famous Royal Air Force church), stood a square, classical, stately building whose corridors I often haunted.

Somerset House, an Elizabethan palace fronting the Thames, housed the offices of the Probate and Divorce Registries. Here sat registrars in high-ceilinged former salons, deciding issues of custody and alimony. Here too I wandered for hours, filing divorce petitions, wills and affidavits.

Nearby, across the Strand, rose modern Bush House, another scene of my activities, rendering unto Caesar stamp duty on property transfer deeds. From the bowels of this building the celebrated BBC

World Service sent its welcome radio messages around the world in times of peace and war.

The first public radio broadcast, in the 1920s, went out from a neighbouring building, whilst a decade later and a mile to the west William Baird experimented, and television was born. I worked daily amidst these stones of history, and could not fail to be influenced by them.

With professional examinations happily completed, my apprenticeship ended. I was summoned to the Law Society where, alongside scores of others, in dignified Chancery Lane, with the President's wise words ringing in my ears, I was ceremoniously admitted to the Roll of Solicitors. It seemed grand, important. I was, it appeared, fit to be let loose on the world; adviser, advocate, conveyancer; 25 years old. My career was to begin. I left behind me the warmth of the flickering flames of Leadenhall Street for the cold challenge of the real world.

'Here is £250', said my enterprising mother, 'go and start your own practice'.

And I did.

The Story

But I never should have. Yet at 25, unmarried, unencumbered, a careful diet, I could live off £3 a week. For the first year I did. I needed a desk. Every lawyer has to have a desk, the more imposing the better. I creaked up to the second floor in an old Tudor building in Fleet Street, where a friend rented me a desk, a chair, and a filing cabinet. I became the proud tenant of half a room (and it wasn't a big room). No line marked the frontier, but the other half contained a further desk, chair, filing cabinet, and tenant. My friend was a good landlord.

Thus equipped, I sat back and awaited clients. Those who promised to patronise this young, new firm never came. Others, of whose existence I knew nothing, did. By the end of the first year I had made such progress that I became the proud tenant of the whole room, with two of everything and one telephone. I began to eat.

Case No. 1 was a young woman and her aunt who were opening a dress shop. The young woman and I have been happily married for years. She had no idea she was my first client.

The 1950s was the age of characters. Below me in Fleet Street was Prince Henry's Room, panelled as it had been three and a half centuries earlier in honour of a scion of the House of Stuart. There Julian Franklyn, writer, historian, held his heraldry classes. He tried to interest me, but I never mastered the complexities of escutcheons, tinctures and blazons. I understood, though, the significance of or and argent: I had need of them. The gaunt figure of Julian striding the Strand, tieless, careless of dress (apart from his perpetual dark blue beret) was a sight as intriguing as the man himself.

A contrasting character was Ronald Thomas Archibald (his first names by which I always referred to him). Once met, he was never forgotten. He possessed a massive leonine head, sparkling, cold, blue eyes, slightly curled mouth, and a personality that exuded super-abundant self-confidence. He had stood as a parliamentary candidate but had withdrawn when some unexplained episode in his life was about to be disclosed. He seemed to be on first name terms with the Cabinet and most MPs. At times I felt he was running the country.

He told me of his sons. He was giving them a good education. He was proud of them. He spoke little of his daughter. He masterminded 91 separate private companies, at least one of which creditors were trying to liquidate weekly. For a year I spent most Mondays in the Companies Court negotiating adjournments.

Robert Thomas Archibald had a standard procedure. When pressed to the limit he paid one-third of a debt. If the creditor went ahead and liquidated the company, the creditor had to account back to the liquidator for cash received within a stated period. Many creditors left the field, feeling that one-third was better than nothing. I began to learn what sang-froid really meant. He was on a knife-edge, a cliff-edge, daily, yet remained cool, calm, unhurried, optimistic.

This extraordinary individual, long since departed from our world, has continued to exert his baleful influence. His son, author John Le Carré, has described him pointedly and accurately in *The Perfect Spy*.

For some reason I began to get Polish clients. I wonder if they knew that both my parents had been born in their country. Many of them had fought with distinction in the Second World War, but refused to return to the motherland and suffer under communism.

They set up communal organisations, clubs, societies, in Britain to maintain their culture. They became a well-integrated minority.

One, an estate agent, challenged me to raise funds for a purchaser of a property, half of which was let to a controlled tenant who paid a very low rent, and could remain, as the law then was, until death, and beyond.

I liked challenges. This was a tough one. Strolling along the Strand I noticed a sign indicating one of the smaller building societies which then flourished, long before the law in 1962 brought order to a barely-controlled market.

Building societies had begun in the 19th century as terminating societies. A group of people got together, saved together, helped put up homes, and, when the group was fully housed, the society terminated. Some people, however, thought it might be a good idea to keep going, take investments from the public, and lend the money to a wider range of home-buyers. Thus began a mammoth movement, typically English. In like fashion many other movements originated in this extraordinary country from small beginnings, trade unions to freemasonry, cricket to co-operatives, football to friendly societies.

I took my courage in my hands, walked in, and found myself in a counting house, with high stool, high collars, *et al.* I was back in the world of Charles Dickens – the Cheeryble Brothers. Furniture and décor had surely survived the wreck of Bleak House. I was met by a short, rotund, smiling manager, watch-chain glistening across bursting waistcoat – Pickwick himself. He looked at me, took pity, and gave a loan. Estate agents and mortgage brokers thereafter swarmed around.

It was at this early stage of my £3-per-week (but gently rising) career that I was invited to become an employer. I must admit I also had temptations. Some sharp, unqualified gentlemen had offered me £100 a week, a fortune in those pre-inflationary days, if they could use my name for an office they were opening. Money was important, but not that important.

However I did become an employer. My employee was a Trinidadian. He had played cricket and football for his country, was a member of the Royal Choral Society, had sung on the West End stage, and was already married with a family. He worked as a typist. Joffre Cumming-Bart asked if he could work for me, despite knowledge of my meagre income. Apart from my father, he was the most honest and upright man I have ever known. When my wife (case No. 1), and I (also a case) went on honeymoon in October 1954, I gave Joffre authority to do whatever he wished with anything I possessed in the world. My trust in him was implicit.

He joined me on a hope and a prayer. Prayer was appropriate, since he was a staunch Roman Catholic. For the next 25 years he regaled me with every encyclical that Rome issued. I became one of the best-educated Jews in Catholic doctrine. He had qualities I did not possess. We became a good team and friends for life. He opened up for me the world of the West Indians who had then started to enter Britain in large numbers.

At the end of the second year in Fleet Street I moved to more 'commodious premises', as they say – one large chamber, which I converted into three smaller rooms. The vendor was a gnarled boxing promoter, one Harry Levine. He could have emerged from the set of *Guys and Dolls*. He insisted, as part of the deal, that I had two free tickets to a world boxing fight he was promoting at Olympia in London. I went, and spent most of the time gaping open-mouthed at the ferocious antics of the audience, cheering on their surrogate gladiators, who covered the ring with gore and blood. Only once since have I ever set foot in such a brutalising establishment.

I also acquired, with my large room, a receptionist who, when not answering the phone, sighed longingly over a picture of the young one of them all – Cliff Richard (later Sir Cliff). My secretary, another character, was a youthful 70 year-old. She never minced her words and knew the world, having been a chorus girl in earlier days. As she lay in her hospital bed dying, Joffre and I asked her if she needed anything. Her reply, 'Yes, a bottle of brandy', which we promptly delivered.

Armed as I was with desks, rooms, and clients, I yet lacked a library. A lawyer had to have law books, but they were expensive. I solved the problem by using the best law library in London – that of The Law Society itself. Frequently, in mid-afternoon, my very own professional body provided chapter and verse for my cases. In winter, I often tiptoed into the great coffee-room and beheld the serried ranks of senior partners, fast asleep in their deep leather armchairs before a blazing fire. Disraeli's description of the Opposition front bench as 'a row of exhausted volcanoes' came to mind.

Being one who has preferred the pursuit of happiness to that of wealth, I was fascinated by the lengths men and women would go to in the hunt for money. Feelings ran especially high after the contents of a will were made known following a death. To this day I can still see the fierce, hate-filled faces of two brothers who accused their sister of murdering their mother to lay hold of her estate. They really believed she had committed the crime. People become irrational, worst instincts rise to the surface. The poor mother, from way above, probably looked down on the three of them with tears in her eyes.

Often incredible plans were devised to cash in. One of them led to the famous Number One Court at the Old Bailey, where I was destined to become involved in many cases. A man took out an accident and sickness policy. He then suffered two 'accidents', was away from work for four weeks and three weeks respectively, produced doctor's certificates, concocted by him, and proceeded to collect a sum equivalent at the time to around £100,000.

He had insured himself for the same risk with 23 companies, perfectly lawful. He had an accomplice, who backed up his statements and claims. No one would have known, or queried a single claim, had two insurance men not met in a City pub, as they were wont to do, and compared some claims they had in hand. This led to probing by the redoubtable City police. The two men involved received remarkably moderate sentences, even more remarkably reduced on appeal, despite their attempts at forgery and conspiracy.

I was so impressed with the Detective Sergeant's handling of the case that I wrote to his superiors praising him. I was delighted to hear, some time later, of his promotion to Inspector, and subsequently to Commander. The police have a difficult job to keep abreast of society's villains. When they succeed, and act in the highest traditions of their profession, commendation is in place.

This case was my first experience of materialistic 'Essex man', later to become part, unjustly no doubt, of our linguistic and political vocabulary.

Fleet Street and the Strand then possessed a number of popular, indeed celebrated, hostelries – The George, El Vino, The Cock, The Cheshire Cheese – wherein lawyers and journalists drank each other's health, and pumped each other for information and copy over a never-ending flow of alcohol. I frequently observed emerging Bardolphs, lighting the way ahead.

My move to Wardour Street in Soho, with the aid of Mr Levine, produced a new crop of characters. The pub names changed. Now it was The Grafton, The Swiss House, The Intrepid Fox – the world subsequently delineated by Jeffrey Bernard. There were many Sohos. It was a village in the midst of a city, a gourmet's dream, with every kind of restaurant and delicatessen. It was also the centre of the film world.

Soho – originally a hunting cry like tally-ho – was then the centre of the new rising coffee-bar world. Young performers, twanging guitars and vocal chords, inhabited them, waiting to be discovered. Tommy Steele was.

Soho was more though. We had a Soho Fair, Soho Beauty Queen, Soho Waiters' Race. Poor struggling authors could sit in Torino's in Old Compton Street for hours, out of the cold, for the price of a coffee. Some later became famous.

Characters continued to walk into the office. A well-known actor and his syndicate bought a racehorse, on which they planned to lose money to set off against their high film contract income. Unhappily for them, the horse kept winning.

An idiosyncratic professor sat down, turned on his recording machine, from which emanated all he wished to tell me, then got up and left. He had been a Brigadier in British Intelligence. Himmler, the Nazi monster, had died in his arms, or so he told me – the arms of a Jew. His experiences in the war had unhinged his mind. Sadly he did not survive for long.

A woman who had won the football pools threw caution to the winds. At last she could achieve her ambition of training racehorses. She spent so wildly that, before long, I was trying to persuade bailiffs not to break down the barricades she had erected around her Yorkshire home.

A client paid a bill with three paintings – one of them was signed 'Gainsborough'. The National Gallery told me the painter didn't sign his paintings. Still, it was of his school, and the client was quite happy – his loft had become tidier.

A 21-year-old Scotsman walked into my office and said he was about to open a men's clothing shop in a run-down, drab, semi-slum street in the West End, known then as the home of a specialist pipe and tobacco retailer. The street, a leftover from the 18th century, hid shabbily behind Oxford and Regent Streets. That was the start of my long link with the phenomenon that was Carnaby Street, and a movement that revolutionised men's clothing.

I confronted an evil in the land: a man named Rachmann, a word synonymous with rapacious landlordism. At first I could not believe anyone could stoop so low in terrorising tenants. I fought him tooth and nail, and almost got him committed to prison, from which he was only saved by his brilliant advocate, Sebag Shaw. If only I had succeeded!

On the other hand, I advised delightful people like celebrated photographer Laelia Goehr, who, as a lifelong friend, not only produced wonderful studies of my children, but also took me behind the scenes at concert rehearsals as she captured the moods of principal performers with her Roliflex.

Laelia's photographs of famous musicians and composers – she spoke all their languages – from Stravinsky to her son Alexander, captured the ecstasy and intensity of the world of music with piercing and artistic perception. Her camera talked, and painted, and felt.

Those few years, those early days, were my real apprenticeship. I learned so much from my clients and cases. I had no degree, had not been to college, but the people I met, the issues I dealt with, the manifold experiences and challenges I faced, were my colleges, my degrees, my universities. They taught me perhaps more than I could have learned in more sober, ordered, and distinguished establishments. Above all those early days were fun. The world was growing, and I was growing with it. It was a time of camaraderie, excitement, and creativity, emerging from the rationing, austerity and drabness of the 'export or die' late 1940s. The 1950s had their own lively character and characters. It was a good time for a young lawyer to face the world, especially the throbbing, exciting world that was London.

Chapter II

Do You Reckon These Two?

Introduction

To those who can remember, the 1960s in Britain were years of release. While the United States was occupied with the murder of a President and civil rights marches, France had rioting students, and Russia and Eastern Europe were frozen in a rigid, corrupt and inefficient totalitarianism, the British, or at least Londoners, were having a ball, out on an iridescent spree.

It was the noisiest of times, the whackiest of times. Everything stiff and formal was behind us; everything lovely and happy ahead of us. The Beatles twanged out a new, engaging electronic sound – the new hymns of youth. Coffee bars sprouted in Soho, the rendezvous for the 'with-it' generation.

Carnaby Street, with whose origin and development I was intimately engaged as adviser throughout the decade, became a by-word for fashion, design and colour, freed from the shackles of Savile Row, exploding with novelty and verve, sending its message of exciting innovation around the world. Cliff Richard sang 'The Young Ones'. The world was our oyster. There was nothing beyond our reach. Peace unto you, brother, and now also to you, sister. It was, of course, a colourful bubble that burst a decade later.

Yet alongside this carefree scene another, grimmer world existed.

From the 1950s, tens of thousands of West Indians had poured into the mother country for which they had great affection. They had been raised on her history, literature, and religion. They had volunteered and fought for her defence in the 1940s. Many had died.

They migrated from the hillsides of Jamaica, the towns of Trinidad and Barbados, the plains of Guyana, from little islands up and down the sunny blue Caribbean. They left a wonderful climate and exotic scenery in search of jobs. Officialdom welcomed them in hospitals, factories, and public transport. But at other levels, problems of adjustment arose, especially as the newcomers congregated in overcrowded, run-down, inner-city tenements. No problem was more significant and more deadly in its long-term effect than their escalating confrontation with the forces of law and order, most notably the police.

The West Indian loved music, noise, parties, standing about in the street, direct conversation, and making observations that were lively and often irreverent – features of a warm climate. The police stood for order, respect for authority, 'Move along there please', 'Don't answer back', and short haircuts. Many had a poor opinion of the immigrants, whom they saw through imperially-tinted eyes. Both sides felt challenged. Deportation could easily follow conviction. Vagrancy laws, 150 years old, were invoked.

A few officers felt the dark-skinned residents were easy pickings in the surge for promotion. The powers-that-be in New Scotland Yard neither knew, nor understood, the internal cancer of racism that was spreading at the grass roots. There were areas of London that became 'no go' areas, not for the police, but for West Indians, who feared an inevitable prosecution if they set foot in certain parts of the city. This tense situation was largely unknown to the joyous, bubbling world existing alongside it nor to the mass of ordinary, commuting, law-abiding suburbanites.

A number of *causes célèbres* emerged in the courts. They received their first public ventilation in a famous TV programme in 1968, *Cause for Concern*. I had been involved as lawyer in most of the cases highlighted for public viewing, and, as such, spent much of my time on and off the programme, trying to make peace between two intensely indignant sets of opponents.

One case, in particular, illustrates the tension of the sixties, whose memory and mythology has bedevilled subsequent decades. Many of my clients became good friends, and the two men I defended in this case so long ago have remained close to me over the years, both subsequently achieving judicial eminence.

The Story

The telephone rang at home one Sunday morning. At the other end was the voice of Sir Learie Constantine, High Commissioner for Trinidad and Tobago in London. I was doing what I usually did at weekends: a bit of gardening, playing football with my sons in the park, reading, watching television, seeing friends and family – the usual things. For the High Commissioner to ring at such a time, however, was unusual.

The name Constantine may mean little to many, but to fellow Trinidadians he was a hero; to cricketers the world over a living legend, one of the greatest all-rounders the game had ever produced. He was adored in Lancashire where, apart from his welfare work, he played for local teams. He was the Babe Ruth, Jack Nicklaus or Bobby Charlton of his sport.

To me he was one of the greatest men I have ever known. Bursting with character and integrity, he was never afraid to stand up for the rights of his people. He and Frank Worrell, the famous West Indies cricket captain, were two men I admired immensely. Constantine, the first West Indian to sit in the House of Lords, once told me of the group he had formed with Sir Hugh Wooding, later Chief Justice of Trinidad, called the 'Love Your Parents Club'. They wanted to emphasise family life and respect by children for their elders. That was the quality of these men and the society from which they came.

Yet why a call at the weekend? What was so urgent? He explained. Two young Trinidadians, working and studying in Britain, had been arrested by the police, and were, at that moment, locked up in a cell at Hampstead Police Station. Learie Constantine, himself a member of the Bar, did not want them to remain in custody, or to be unrepresented. He knew of the quality of the two men, and their families. He could not conceive that they had committed any offence. In fact they had denied involvement in anything criminal. Would I visit them in that north-west London police station in which they were ensconced and help them? I agreed to go at once. I dropped everything, even playing football.

That phone call ushered in a series of events that not only later made legal history, but involved a host of legal luminaries, including Dingle Foot, Tom Kellock, Sebag Shaw, Peter Rawlinson – a future attorney-general and future judges and parliamentarians.

In the police station I learned what had happened. Two plain clothes officers had arrested Desmond and George for trying to take and drive away parked motor vehicles; not an earth-shaking offence, but, if proved, one that could have destroyed their careers.

It seemed a wholly implausible accusation. Both were in their twenties. Desmond had been admitted as a barrister and was an outstanding tennis player and sportsman. George was a qualified teacher and Olympic athlete, as well as a highly advanced black belt in judo. Both had university degrees. Both came from good families, had attended well-known schools, had never been in conflict with the law anywhere. Both were at the start of what could be distinguished careers.

What were they doing sitting there in a police station, charged with attempting to take away other people's cars? They did not know, but what stuck in their gullet and shocked them was a single action by one of the police officers. Whilst noting their possessions on the police sheet – normal procedure – he had dropped a set of car keys onto the desk which he said had been found on the accused; a set of keys neither Desmond nor George had ever set eyes on before. They refused to sign the sheet admitting possession of the keys.

There is a certain psychology among many citizens, especially innocent ones, who find themselves accused of some crime and placed under the control of uniformed officers: a mixture of respect for authority and disbelief in what was happening.

It is a situation so unusual, so fraught with tension and confusion, that often statements are made, even signed, that bear no relation to reality. But for innocent men, deprived of their liberty, to witness false evidence being concocted before their eyes, and by officers of a force with a reputation they had been brought up to respect, was breathtaking, unbelievable, sickening.

In the 1960s, good, solid citizens, reared on a television diet of *Dixon of Dock Green*, where the police officer was friendly, caring, upright, and honest, could never believe that the force contained men who could so deliberately pervert the course of justice.

My immediate aims at the police station were to prevent any statement being made by the accused, in their state of shocked indignation; not to allow the issue of the keys to prevent their release; and above all to obtain bail so that they need spend no further time under legal constraint. These aims I managed to achieve.

It had been cold, dark, bleak and wintery, with a biting wind and snow in the air the evening they had been arrested. The two figures, bundled in anoraks, shoulders hunched, hands in pockets, had been walking southwards north of Finchley Road Underground station.

Finchley Road is a major artery, commencing close to the

cricketing holy of holies, Lords, and ending five miles to the north at the North Circular Road, one of London's main arterial routes circumnavigating the central boroughs. Finchley Road is constantly busy with transport, well lit, a bus route, with cars frequently parked on both sides. Pedestrians were easily visible by the dwellers of the numerous flats and apartments above the lengthy parades of shops. Distances and timing, as it later transpired, become important.

The prosecution presented their evidence to the magistrates' court and supplied us with written statements of the case. We prepared for the hearing in Number One Court at the Old Bailey, where many famous trials had taken place.

We had prepared well. I examined, cross-examined, and probed George and Desmond endlessly before they stood in the witness box. After all, if the jury believed them, the implication was that the police officers were lying. There was no question of innocent mistake. It was a formidable task. In the 1960s, juries were far more likely to believe two police detectives than two black West Indians.

The police gave evidence. They described how they had observed George and Desmond walking slowly along the pavement for a long distance, trying the door handles of car after car. Dingle Foot, for the defence, questioned them from first-hand knowledge. He, myself, and the two Trinidadians had walked up and down the relevant stretch of road again and again, timing ourselves. It had been a rare sight; this distinguished QC, formerly a prominent MP, and his legal entourage, marching along the busy road, checking distances and holding stop watches.

The preparation paid off. The officers had never suspected their evidence would be shown to be nonsense, impossible as to both distance and timing.

Desmond and George made a good impression by the transparent truthfulness of their words and their courteous, dignified bearing. Not only did they not have any car keys on them, neither of them owned a car. Desmond could not even drive. Both told how they had suddenly been bundled into a telephone box by two short police officers. Had they, both six-footers, retaliated, they knew they would have been charged with assault, as had happened to many others. Had the officers known that George was trained by England's judo coach, they would have been a shade more careful.

Both defendants confirmed that, when first stopped, suddenly and for no reason, they were amazed at the allegations. Both heard one officer ask the other, 'Do you reckon these two?'. The other had nodded his assent. The accused could have been any two poor, vulnerable West Indians, picked on, dragged through the courts, contending hopelessly against the combined evidence of prosecution and police. How many lives and careers had been blighted in this way in other cases?

But they had not apprehended two ordinary men. They had arrested two highly-educated, articulate and courageous Trinidadians, a people noted for their forthrightness, for 'telling it as it is'.

The other mistake the officers made was to rouse the ire of Sir Learie. He it was who, in the 1940s, had dragged a famous hotel group through the courts because they would not honour their contract with him when they discovered that he, their guest, was a coloured man. After that, no hotel dishonoured a booking because the guest was not white-skinned.

For the defence of Desmond and George we had mobilised resources equal to those of the prosecution. The two officers, falsely arresting two likely-looking victims on a freezing night, would have thought twice had they had an inkling of what they would face.

The High Commissioner, his country's ambassador at the Court of St. James, did not worry about political niceties when human rights were at stake. He was in court when the jury retired, and remained there after the jury brought in a verdict of not guilty. He smiled broadly.

The scene changed rapidly to the High Court where civil cases were heard. Peter Rawlinson asked another jury for exemplary damages for malicious prosecution and false imprisonment. I watched with fascination as the women jurors sat entranced and bewitched by the eloquence of this tall, handsome, distinguished advocate.

Counsel for the police, Sebag Shaw, later Lord Justice Shaw, equally distinguished, was heard to mutter as he left for the court on the final day, 'Now I know what the Gadarene swine felt like'.

The jury found for Trinidad and awarded the plaintiffs record damages for the particular wrongs they had suffered. The Law Courts erupted with journalists. Full reports appeared in the newspapers in Britain and abroad. George and Desmond's features were seen by millions on the nation's television screens, and we all celebrated in proper fashion.

George, impressed by his experiences, went on to read for the Bar and was admitted as a barrister. Desmond became a noted advocate, both in Trinidad and England. Both married, had families, and lived normal lives. What a debt they owed to a man who would not see his fellow-countrymen humiliated, and who placed human rights above diplomatic equivocation.

Yet why had police officers, who had put their own careers in jeopardy by their irresponsible action, behaved so miserably? I was puzzled. I enquired further. Did they need to add to their quiver of successful prosecutions in order to obtain promotion? Was it racism at work? Or was it an assessment that certain groups of immigrants, coloured ones especially, were the easiest to exploit? Were they cynical about their superiors, or indeed sanctioned by the timorousness or myopia of those same superiors, and the system they were supposed to serve?

A simple, yet prosaic reason emerged for their behaviour. They were as cold and as frozen on that bitter night as the two they had 'reckoned' and arrested. They decided not to patrol the street, not to do their allotted duty. They spent most of the evening in a local restaurant, emerging at a point close to the scene of the arrest.

They sought to justify, in their reports, how they had spent their time, and so concocted a story about following suspects along the highway. Without checking distances and timing at all, they had proceeded to arrest, on the spot, two men who looked unlikely to cause trouble. It was a *folie à deux* of an unusual kind. It failed because of a resolute defence, attention to the minutest details, and the resolve of a rare man who fought for justice and human dignity.

Chapter III

A Night for St Patrick

Introduction

The Irish are a wonderful people, yet have had a terrible time of it. They were unlucky to occupy an island close to Britain when the English were in their most imperial mood. The result has been famine, emigration, and violence. The result has also been independence, the rule of law, democracy, the English language, no passports to Britain, and a vote in British elections.

There are so many contradictions in the Irish-English relationship. The Irish are among the greatest practitioners of the English language. They produced Swift, Burke, Synge, Wilde, and Shaw. They have such an easy fluency, such a mastery of words. One day one of the famous Behan family, Dominic, walked into my office and regaled me with a problem, described with a rare accumulation of graphic phrases. At a later date I represented a Catholic school, led by an Irish headteacher who likewise combined ease of presentation with abundant charm.

The Republic of Ireland holds almost four million Irish, yet, in addition, close to half that number continue to live in Britain, making them the largest ethnic minority in the UK. There is also the large and active Irish Diaspora, from New Zealand to New York.

In 1990 the Home Secretary invited me to become a commissioner at the Commission for Racial Equality, the body entrusted with administering Britain's race relations laws. I agreed, and found the work fascinating, the CRE's efforts valuable and significant, but the output of paper unbelievably voluminous.

However, what was represented to us at the Commission by an Irish research body was the proposition that the Irish in Britain were the most disadvantaged and discriminated-against ethnic group in the country, having the largest number of alcoholics, jobless, homeless, prison and mental hospital inmates of all the minorities. I confess I was not the only commissioner surprised at this information, having met many Irish in London who had made such good progress up the social and economic ladder.

But there is no doubt that whilst the Republic is a peaceful place, especially its beautiful countryside, there is an element in whom violence simmers just below the surface and explodes periodically. One such explosion landed Danny in my office.

The Story

The public house, or English pub, as an institution, has never been part of my heritage. When my mother emigrated from Kalisz in Poland to England at the beginning of the century, she was shocked by the sight that met her in east London, where most Jews had settled. The streets were littered with drunks lying helpless in gutters, or on pavements. Alcohol caused unspeakable violence within families. Pubs, rather than homes, were the centre of social life as, to a large extent, they still are.

My mother was horrified. She wished to return immediately to Eastern Europe notwithstanding the poverty, racism, and persecution she had left behind. However, she remained and later married my father, who himself had arrived in London from Poland, as a 13-year-old, on the very day of Queen Victoria's Diamond Jubilee.

Love of alcohol has a long tradition in England. The popular phrase in the 18th century was 'drunk for a penny, dead drunk for tuppence'. Gin, known as 'mother's ruin', and the whole ethos of the music hall from 1880 to 1914 ('a little of what you fancy does you good'), all contributed to a positive image for alcohol.

The impoverished working class, living in residential barracks, found an outlet for sorrows and frustrations, as well as social support, in the pub. 'General' William Booth tried to provide a very different outlet in his redeeming Salvation Army. It was in the East End that his army began to march, and still marches, to fight the evil of alcoholism.

The man in my office seeking my help told me of an incident in a pub. Drinking in a public house weekly, sometimes daily, was second nature to him. I had to get into his mind, his experience, as I doubt if I set foot in a pub more than a few times a year, and then usually to eat. His world was not my world, his ways not my ways, but, as in all my cases, I had to get close to his lifestyle to understand him.

I also had to visit the scene of the incident, to re-create the course of events. This bore fruit. Something invariably emerged from an on-site visit which no written statement, no discussion in an office, could anticipate or contemplate. Even witnesses emerged, as if from nowhere, when it was known someone was snooping about.

Danny faced a serious assault charge. Various laws defined gradations of severity. Common assault was not so serious and was dealt with daily by magistrates. Actual bodily harm was more substantial. Causing grievous bodily harm, at the time, was about as grave an assault charge as one could face. It was the last of these Danny had to answer.

Apparently the fracas had occurred on St Patrick's Day. The pub was in the Paddington-Kilburn area, an inner northwestern suburb where many Irish families lived. Danny was a regular. He knew the other regulars. Pints of beer flowed down eager throats that night, contributing to the beer belly so typical of big drinkers.

As inhibitions disappeared, voices were raised, minor points of difference became major issues in an increasingly heated and noisy confrontation; someone prodded somebody else, who responded with a retaliatory push; others joined in, took sides, and, in a twinkling of an eye, chairs and bottles were flying through the air, faces bleeding, bodies slumped to the floor, and general chaos reigned. The pub became a battlefield. Only when police and ambulance arrived did the explosion subside.

This was the account I received from Danny, from the prosecution papers, and from my own visit to the pub, where I talked to the inhabitants of the area.

Many solicitors employ private enquiry agents or investigators. In 1992 I met William Dear, America's self-proclaimed number-one private detective. I read about his cases, his approach. We remained in touch. I have employed many detectives frequently, but, as in other cases, I decided to do my own detective work in this affair. It fascinated me.

The afflicted pub, by the time of my visit, had been restored to some kind of order. It was drab, set in a parade of run-down shops, close to row upon row of undistinguished terrace houses. Behind the frosted glass of the fascia could be seen the traditional pub colours of the day – dirty brown, dirty yellow, and anonymous sepia.

The chairs and tables, at least those that had survived, looked as if they had been similarly used on previous occasions. I sat and ordered a Guinness. I was suitably dressed in an old raincoat. I wanted to know why, in such a mêlée, Danny alone had been charged. The police saw nothing, and may have had difficulty getting clear statements as to responsibility. This emerged from the statements sent to me by the prosecution, which rested on the evidence of one particular person.

I could see, however, why someone had to be prosecuted. The main witness had had 48 stitches in his face. Apparently, the delightful process of combatants honouring the Christian saint, was to hold a beer bottle by its narrow neck, smash it on a bar-edge and then thrust the jagged edge of the remaining section into the face of some unsuspecting colleague. The photographs of the injured man were appalling. Yet in their excited, inebriated state could anyone be sure who had actually caused the injuries – one assailant or several?

Danny, I gathered from my researches, had been picked out and named because of some family-feud totally unrelated to St Patrick or any other saint. The injured witness had not been too keen on naming Danny but members of his family had egged him on. There was no doubt he was injured, no doubt that Danny had injured someone, been injured himself in fact; no doubt that Danny and the witness had had words, had each assaulted someone.

As I questioned people who had been in the pub on that fateful night, and others who knew the principal participants, I realised that, though my home was not so far from theirs, I could have been living on another planet. So many different worlds live together in one city, unaware of each other; different lifestyles, beliefs, values, behaviour. This is why good community relations is such a delicate and difficult art. Each group thinks its own beliefs and way of life are the norm. Those of other groups often represent a standing challenge.

I had come across, in Danny's case, a world of prolonged nightly drinking in a pub; of large, poor families, wives old beyond their years, unemployment and casual building work; a world in which violence was in no way exceptional.

This was the picture that emerged at the Old Bailey. Not much was in dispute – the fighting, the injuries, the photographs. What had to be established was whether Danny had deliberately caused those awful injuries, with intent, to the witness on whom the prosecution so signally relied.

Prosecuting counsel, short, plump-faced, bewigged and begowned, opened the case confidently, distributed the photographs to the jury, who, after seeing them, glared aggressively at the man in the dock. On paper it looked like an open and shut case.

After giving his personal details in the witness box, the questioning went something like this:

Prosecution (pointing to the dock) You know the accused?
Witness Yes.
Prosecution Did you speak to him in the pub on the night you were injured?
Witness Yes.
Prosecution Were you arguing with him?
Witness No. We were quite friendly.
Shuffling of prosecution papers
Prosecution Well, did you have a difference of opinion with him then?
Witness No more than with anyone else.
Prosecution There was a fight in the pub while you were there?
Witness (enthusiastically) Yes. Quite a fight.
Prosecution You were there just to have a drink. You didn't want to get involved in the fight, did you?
Witness Not likely. I joined in.
Reddening of prosecution face, sniggering in gallery, judge furrows his brow.
Prosecution You were attacked weren't you?
Witness Yes.
Prosecution You reacted?
Witness Yes.
Prosecution But you didn't use more force than was reasonably necessary to defend yourself?
Witness Goodness, yes. I laid about me left and right, and gave more than I got.
Increased shuffling of papers, prosecution head sinking deeper into neck.
Prosecution (pointing to Danny) You remember him assaulting you with a bottle?
Witness Can't really tell if it was him. There were so many hitting each other, bottles, fists, chairs... whatever.

Prosecution You mean you can't tell members of the jury that it was the accused who caused your injuries?
Witness Can't remember who stuck the bottle in my face.
Prosecution Well, having been injured, you wanted to get out of the fight as quickly as possible?
Witness No, why should I?
Prosecution looks desperate, looks appealingly to judge.
Judge (to Prosecution) Are you relying on this witness?
Prosecution Yes, my lord.
Judge Have you any other direct witnesses?
Prosecution No, my lord.
Judge Then would you like to consider your position?
Prosecution in a huddle – whispers, grim faces.
Prosecution (looks up) I am instructed, my lord, not to proceed, and to withdraw the prosecution.
Judge That sounds, if I may say so, very sensible.
Judge directs jury to bring in a not guilty verdict.
Exeunt all, prosecution, defence, witnesses and jury.

Of course any lawyer worth his salt will immediately notice that few of the above questions would be permitted. 'Leading questions', he would exclaim. Funny thing, leading questions. The cross-examiner can ask almost what he likes, can make the most outrageous suggestions, such as, 'I put it to you that you are a liar'. No one will stop him. But counsel questioning his own witness is confined in a legal straitjacket.

What a way to get at the truth! One day the nonsense of leading questions will come to an end, as it already has in coroners' courts and some tribunals.

Early in my career, if a husband and wife got together and agreed on a divorce, they wouldn't be granted a divorce. It was collusion, connivance – great absolute sins. After 1967 the sin ceased to be venal, mortal, or even a sin at all. Vice became a virtue. The law stood on its head, just as I predict it will as regards the current 'crime' of asking leading questions. But back to St Patrick.

Outside the court it dawned on me how resentful the parties had been. Here was St Patrick's night, a good excuse for a drink and a lively time. How mean it was for the police to intervene and spoil a good evening's fun. As for courts and written statements, well, as you know, things can change.

It is believed prosecuting counsel left the court muttering under his breath, 'The Irish, I'll never understand them'.

Danny was pleased and went off to celebrate, probably to the same pub, accompanied by a crowd of friends, the crown's main witness probably among them.

I sympathised with the prosecution. It was another world. One day I would understand it.

Chapter IV

Sex and the Single School-Girl

Introduction

M y first office was in Fleet Street, in one of the few Tudor buildings to escape the Great Fire of London in 1666. The stairs had, through the centuries, keeled over at such an angle that clients felt either sea-sick or slightly drunk on reaching their elevated destination. I soon repaired from there to Wardour Street in the wicked heart of central Soho, once a hunting-ground for fox-hunters, but, in my time, a hunting-ground for, or by, young ladies of the streets.

Eventually I escaped to the greenery of Lincoln's Inn Fields, home of legal respectability, Sir John Soanes Museum, Adam ceilings in exquisite Georgian houses, seat (at the time) of the Land Registry and the Public Trustee, and former residence of the only British Prime Minister to have been assassinated. Of course, the thought has often crossed people's minds in relation to other Ministers, but this country is a tolerant nation and disposes of leaders through the ballot box, or, failing that, the media.

All three of my offices were situated in neighbourhoods with certain sexual overtones at one time or another. Dr Samuel Johnson lived just off Fleet Street, where accosting was not unknown, according to James Boswell – no mean accoster himself.

Lincoln's Inn, prim and proper in the 1960s, had not always been thus. In a less salubrious age, the Fields harboured a host of prostitutes, at least according to indefatigable diarist, Samuel Pepys, who had a discerning eye, and was ever repairing to bed.

Sexual cases, however, did not often wend my way. I had defended in abortion cases, where the accused were humane people seeking to help young women in trouble before the abortion laws were changed.

A strange case, however, did walk in one day, sat down and told a slightly unbelievable story; one that amused my staff, all of whom showed a sudden and strange desire to exert themselves on this case far beyond the call of duty.

The Story

This almost nondescript person (if any human being dare be so described) sought my help. He was perplexed. He lived a normal sort of life, was an average man. He earned a living working on building sites. There was little to be said for or against him, except that he had avoided any previous conflict or contact with the law. He kept himself to himself. His CV or obituary would say little except that he was young, unmarried, a man of no exceptional achievement. There are such people, and the world could not keep spinning without them.

He was in considerable trouble. Parents in a respectable London suburb had complained to the police that he had been interfering with their 13- and 14-year-old daughters, who attended a local school close to his place of work.

This could have been a serious situation. Sexual intercourse with a girl under the age of 16 was an absolute crime to which there was no defence. Fortunately this was not the charge. Nor was he accused of rape. I had been involved in the defence of rape cases. I had also helped victims of rape, shattered women, who had had to stand in a witness box while a supercilious counsel suggested that they had consented, even encouraged, intercourse.

I doubt whether defending barristers, doing what they see as their duty, realise the horror of such suggestions to a woman whose body has been invaded, whose whole world has been shaken, whose self-respect has been toppled, whose future, as the result of one aggressive act, has become uncertain and insecure.

On the other hand, the man is not always the guilty party. At the same time as penning these lines, I am investigating a case in which a man is lingering in prison for a rape which I am convinced he never perpetrated, all linked to how reliable evidence as to DNA really is.

But the worried man who sat before me faced somewhat lesser charges than rape, involving familiarity with the girls and their bodies. He admitted the charges to some extent, but said no action had ever been initiated by him. I wondered. He had no idea of the age of the girls. They seemed so well-developed. They had incited him. I had heard such stories before, but a solicitor is neither judge nor jury, and presents to the court the story given to him.

As I looked through the prosecution papers, I realised the police had taken statements from the girls in the presence of their parents – as was their duty – which, on the face of it, showed a good case for the prosecution. Yet it was only part of the story, as I soon learned.

What emerged was unexpected. Those were the days shortly after *Lady Chatterley's Lover* had been an issue in the courts. Everyone was reading D.H. Lawrence's famous story. There was nothing like prosecuting a book to boost its sales.

The schoolgirls were not exempt from the general interest in the story. They were also not exempt from a particular interest in my client, a building worker. As they passed his site daily they taunted and teased him, flaunted themselves before him, even exposed themselves. It was a campaign of sexual incitement.

I was no authority on what 14-year-old girls talk to each other about. I wondered whether there was any substance in his explanations. Was the client blaming the girls, believing it was the only chance he had?

My doubts were soon dispelled. Somehow the girls had discovered his home address. They had begun sending him letters of sexual explicitness, with such vivid proposals and suggestions as would make an experienced lawyer blush. What effect they had on a strong, virile building worker, I daren't imagine.

That was not all though. There followed a postal barrage to him of cuttings from *Lady Chatterley's Lover*, describing the developing physical relationship between the Lady and her gardener. Mere man that the worker was, he responded – up to a point only – and found himself in court.

My excessively enthusiastic staff decided they had to pinpoint the extracts precisely, and searched and re-searched the book, noting the relevant pages, sometimes concealing the book within the ample folds of the Rules of the Supreme Court.

As the defence unfolded, producing irrefutable, illuminating, inflammatory exhibits, the faces of the girls' parents, originally indignant, changed from disbelief, to incredulity, to anger. The girls shrivelled even more within their seats. Slowly and deliberately the letters were read aloud, in all their heated detail, and Lady

Chatterley inevitably got an airing. By then the heart had gone out of the prosecution, the judge, the jury, and everyone, especially the sad silly girls.

The defendant received some moderate non-custodial sentence. The girls shrunk home. What later transpired between them and their parents must have been equally illuminating, if not explosive.

The case confirmed the view I had always taken – never to rely on written statements, as the prosecution had done, or to prejudge, but to keep an open mind as I encountered the increasingly strange world of our human species.

By the way, the man I defended was a Mr Innocent.

Chapter V

The Tax Man Cometh

or *Cuckoo in the Nest*

Introduction

I read somewhere that we human beings need sleep, not to rest, but to dream. If we do not dream there will be no rest. We are not conscious of the great majority of dreams. A few we remember. Some we read about. The Bible is full of dreams. Jacob, Joseph, Pharoah were full of them. Martin Luther King had a dream.

Today, in our programmed, predestined, conditioned routine, we need an escape, a sense of fantasy. Britain has been blessed with many fantasists. Names roll off the tongue: Lewis Carroll, Edward Lear, A.A. Milne, the radio world of *ITMA* and *The Goon Show* – fantasists all, saying the unexpected, reversing patterns of thought and behaviour to which we are daily accustomed.

Arabs and Persians luxuriated in fantasies, from *A Thousand and One Nights* to an afterlife of eternal pleasure – escapes from reality. The lawyer, like the psychiatrist, is no stranger to stories larger, much larger, than life. Some are sad. Their narrators need special help.

How often have people sat in my office and told me how they watched television programmes directed personally at them; programmes that insulted and defamed them deliberately; them and no one else. The stories were so convincing. The viewers had been hurt to the core of their souls. They wanted to sue at once. We never did. It was a paranoiac fantasy I soon learned to recognise.

Of course the Messiah was also a client. Religious fantasy can take hold of the most harmless of humans and send them soaring into the heavens. When it happens to people en masse there is no telling where it will end – the mass suicide in Guyana in the 1970s, and similar sad episodes in the 1980s and 1990s, or the foundation of a new faith.

It is less dangerous in an individual. For years I received regular letters from a man I had helped in a family problem which had obsessed him, unhinged him. Every letter, marked private and confidential, was signed 'the Messiah'. Each missive was replete with quotations from the Bible – he knew the Books by heart – as well as prophecies of doom. Yet this same man did a normal daily job, normally. Somewhere along the line fantasy took over.

We all need outlets. Fairy stories are fantasy stories. Much of Shakespeare is fantasy. The modern cinema carries us into a world of make-believe. When alone, I confess, I am also a fantasist. How often have I conducted a whole symphony, imagining an orchestra spread before me. Recently my son, out in the street, saw me jumping about in my study. Was I doing exercises? No, just dancing – I adore dancing – imagining I was some latter-day Fred Astaire moving to the tuneful rhythms of Perry Como, a great favourite. Pure fantasy, but how satisfying.

I came across a man who worked in a tax office. He was an ordinary man, but blessed (or cursed) with a rare sense of fantasy. He applied his poetic imagination to prosaic financial assessments and rebates. In the process he caused tremors in the heart of the British tax system.

He was an ordinary man who climbed out of his ordinariness into a world of make-believe; who used an unusual inventiveness for strictly practical and mercenary ends. Thus did I find prose and poetry lodged at the same time in the soul of a tax officer whose needs were pressing, and who found opportunities conveniently close at hand.

The Story

The British Empire was an amazing phenomenon. Nothing like it had been seen before: an expanding British universe, spilling over into all continents and oceans, on which the sun, the moon and the stars of heaven never set. British immigration was perpetual, but into other people's countries. The immigrants began at the top, bringing with them trade, Christianity, straight roads, afternoon tea, and the English common law.

After two world wars in this century, the Empire graduated into the British Commonwealth, and thence into the Commonwealth, a unique association of fifty-three sovereign states, including twenty-seven Republics, inhabited by a billion beings, black, brown and white.

Among them was a brown man who had left his native Pakistan to pan for gold in the streets of London. He came as an immigrant, borne along by the waves of population that swept into post-1945 Britain. For Britain then was an open society. A British subject could move in and out freely. He simply waved his passport and pronounced, in his best imperial accent, '*Civis Britannicus sum*', and in he came. It was only later, after 1962, that immigration and nationality laws proliferated, closing doors, creating confusion and uncertainty, and driving the perplexed into the arms of specialist lawyers, who themselves sat scratching their heads, trying to bring clarity and sense into what seemed to be legislative chaos.

My Pakistani had my sympathy, as he sat in the waiting room. I have always had a sympathy for immigrants. My parents had been immigrants fleeing from Eastern European persecution, arriving in Britain as teenagers, knowing not a word of English, possessing not an English penny. I had been raised in an immigrant community – they are all ghettoes, usually self-imposed for protection – where the common language was not English. When my father sent me out to buy a newspaper, it was for a Yiddish, not an English, journal.

Mine was a typical story, so I knew something of the mentality of the newcomer, the stranger in a strange land. But I had in no way bargained for the kind of mentality that inhabited the inventive head of the man waiting to tell me his tale of woe.

There is a suspense and an apprehension about waiting-rooms. Ancient wisdom has it that we all live in a universal waiting-room. My habit is always to go forth and welcome someone who has patiently waited to see me and take him along to my own room, rather than have him sent impersonally along a corridor.

There he was, sitting quietly but apprehensive, in his forties, average height, black eyes, black hair yielding somewhat to the erosion of time, long arms and large spreading expressive hands, and a peculiar habit of tilting his head as he spoke. In the next few months I got to know him well. He had admirable qualities, especially love for his family. His story, later told publicly (as were most of the stories related in this volume), had a touch of Eastern fantasy. It gradually unfolded as the legal machine got under way.

We have a two-tiered system of dealing with criminal cases. The great majority never go further than the local magistrates' courts, where lay and professional justices administer a vast array of laws, from driving offences to petty thefts and assaults. The more serious cases usually go on to a higher court, a crown court, where witnesses tell their story to the court, judges tell the jury the law, and the jury tell the judge their findings of fact. The press and the media then tell the public.

But, of course, the prosecution, in these serious matters, have to establish at least a *prima-facie* case, so that the time of judge and jury should not be wasted on nonsense. Such ostensible cases used to be presented orally in the lower court, but protests at the resulting delay brought a change in procedure, whereby the prosecution delivered to the defence a dossier of written evidence well before the hearing. The defending lawyer could then decide whether the documents disclosed a *prima-facie* case or not.

As usual, the magistrates' court hearing was greatly shortened, and the battle, if battle there was to be, shifted to the higher court. It also meant that the defence knew most of the prosecution case, without having to reveal its own.

My friend from Pakistan, like so many from that sub-continent, had a feeling for figures, numbers. This could have led him into an accountants' or cashiers' office. Instead, he was welcomed as a clerk by Her Majesty's Inspector of Taxes. The Queen may not have known her new obedient servant, but he worked assiduously, progressed from section to section, until he understood the whole persecutory process that annually, immutably, afflicts the ordinary citizen.

Each tax office administers the assessment of tax in specific areas. There is an internal system of checks and balances to see that the process is not abused, and indeed Britain is blessed with an honest set of administrators. Yet the very words, tax collectors, have something demeaning about them, an echo of Biblical condemnation, the organisation of eager takers from reluctant givers. Could William Pitt the Younger, and later William Gladstone, have ever appreciated what a growth industry they had initiated?

As my tax collecting client worked daily, watching the great inward movement of money in response to the letters and forms that poured out from his office, an idea began to take shape in his lively mind. He never saw it is as guilty idea. He never used that word in all our conversations. Why, he felt, should he not enter into partnership with the Inspector? The latter had a monopoly on tax-collecting. Why should a little free enterprise not penetrate this financial closed shop?

Indeed, in his own sing-song voice, questioning, justifying, throwing out his arms, expressive hands waving, he explained, with a certain pride, and in some detail, his breakaway movement. He had a dry voice, hoarse when excited, but usually undramatic, like his clothes, which contrasted sharply with his sudden bursts of physical agitation.

How could he set up his own personal collecting system within the larger official unit? Using his extensive procedural knowledge, he devised a scheme of unbelievable audacity.

Our gatherers of tax sometimes have to return overpayments to the long-suffering public, which they do with studied reluctance and little sense of urgency. Someone may marry, or have a child, or, sadly, lose a job, or some event occurs that entitles him or her to demand a repayment of a portion of the tax garnered from him. The magic word is rebate. He can call for a rebate – a repayment of some of the money sucked from him by the system.

My friend discovered that, for some obscure reason, people had failed to claim rebates. It happens all the time. People disappear, emigrate. Some want nothing to do with the tax world so that they can sleep at night. Thus, money accumulated in Government hands that should have been in people's pockets. It was unjust, unfair. Why should the state retain money belonging to the hard-working citizen? The state, neither in capitalist nor in communist society, showed any sign of withering away. Neither Marx, nor Spencer, were right. So why not see justice done, and remove from Government hands money to which it was not entitled?

My Pakistani taxman confirmed to me – justified to me – what the police had already discovered. He had found old files stored in dusty cupboards in basements and breathed life into them. In the names of the disappearing citizens he wrote a series of letters claiming rebates. The letters came to him. He wrote back querying the claims. He replied to himself with details. He questioned the details. If no speedy response occurred, he threatened to close the correspondence. If a response came with details, he announced he would check them and give his decision.

The files grew, and grew. Various handwriting styles emerged from different parts of London. The bizarre correspondence continued, until eventually, in most cases, he agreed the rebates claimed, or some lesser sum, though not too much less.

As this procedure proved satisfactory, a new thought arose. Why revive old files only? Why not create new, previously unknown persons, as well as resurrecting the dead, or restoring to the community those long settled in distant lands? Letters began to come into the office, to him, from a new category of claimants, the creation of his 'heat-oppressed brow'. A similar correspondence ensued. With one claimant he became quite angry, reflected in letters doubting the veracity and honesty of the correspondent. Righteous indignation shone through the reply, but the altercation subsided, and the rebate was allowed.

There were problems. Maybe the left hand and the right hand did not know of each other, but there were other hands in the office whose signatures were necessary before cheques were let loose on the world. Somehow these additional signatures were obtained, often routinely given, occasionally justified by the sight of the legitimate-looking correspondence, believing the signatures and induced by assurances received from this highly-regarded, industrious public servant. Months went by, and the Exchequer became leaner.

But what was to happen to the cheques? A plan must be foolproof. Everything must be foreseen. Loose ends were anathema. The payments had to be cleared through banks. Thus ensued a series of friendly visits to widely separated bank managers, and the opening of new accounts, one per cheque. Documentation and specimen signatures abounded. Thousands and thousands of pounds poured through clearing houses, mere flashes in the eye of a computer. Amounts were withdrawn, accounts never overdrawn.

The merry game continued. This prime example of free enterprise prospered, a cuckoo in a tax inspector's nest, despatching a series of golden eggs, until of course the inevitable fateful day of discovery. But how and where could it arise? There were so many possibilities: from the tax office itself, the banks, the claimants' addresses, a slip of the tongue or pen, the appearance of a true claimant, a query of a reference number. The scheme could founder in so many ways.

I ventured further into this man's life. In 1947 he and his family had fled from India into newly-created Pakistan. He came to Britain, later bringing his wife. The family relied on him: many sisters, mother, wife, three unsettled children, daughter requiring a dowry. Everyone looked to him, head of the family, universal provider. The pressure was so great. He had to find a way.

The tax office was his solution. He became the perfect tax officer. Confidential reports of superiors positively glowed. 'His application and wholehearted efforts leave nothing to be desired.' He was on the brink of promotion, this 'likeable popular man who got on with things'.

The future looked assured. Then suddenly by chance, one of the 'dead' claimants came to life. An innocent letter, a search for a file, a puzzled chief inspector, and, lo and behold, a six-year campaign of deception came to light. During all that time our highly trained obedient servants with their systems, their checks and balances, were unable to perceive a haemorrhaging of Her Majesty's revenue in the form of hundreds of rebates sprouting in the hands of a host of equally unsuspecting bank managers.

Her Majesty, I regret to say, missed a great opportunity. Instead of prosecuting this semi-genius, she should have put him in charge of the whole tax structure. His knowledge, his flair, his imagination, were startling. If references for him were required, there they were in court. The Inland Revenue chief investigating officer had said it was 'One of the largest investigations ever undertaken. The accused had shown a remarkably brilliant and inventive mind'. Few tax officers would ever get such a recommendation.

Prosecuting counsel averred, 'The most extensive internal fraud by an employee ever brought to light'.

Commendation indeed for one who thought big. Even Her Majesty's sober judge was moved to a sense of admiration, 'Ingenious, imaginative, thoroughness.'

I have no doubt our voyager from Pakistan rendered a signal service to the Revenue. Great internal procedural changes followed the case, yet not a word of appreciation was expressed. No thanks, no gratitude, in fact just the reverse. The word from the bench was three years in Her Majesty's prison as society's response to such unparalleled ingenuity.

Imagine if he had been promoted, if this rare mind had been harnessed to legitimate ends. We have got it all wrong. The Revenue could have spent a fortune on business systems advisers and still not receive the degree of benefit and insight they would have derived from our man from the East. He worked at the grass roots, not in the tree tops.

Whilst languishing in the depths of prison, he realised how unappreciative his employers had been. The case had been over but a few months when a letter arrived on my desk. He told me about the prison, his family, his wife's illnesses, adding a simple request. As his case had now been settled, he wanted to go about claiming salary for months (number given), superannuation contributions, relief for higher personal allowances (years specified), and (inevitably) refund of tax for all such years. I took a deep, deep breath.

Persistent he was, yet possessed of that rarest of qualities which some call chutzpah. I was tempted to reply, asking if he would prepare the necessary documentation. I could just imagine Her Majesty's face, scanning one more original claim for tax rebate from one of her erstwhile lodgers.

The form, I am sure, would be perfectly, convincingly completed, in whomsoever's name it might appear. It would have been a fascinating exercise. Who knows, as things were, he might even have got a rebate.

Chapter VI

The Consul

Introduction

I have been enormously privileged in my life, not merely in my childhood, my parents, my wife and children, but in the insights I have been vouchsafed into the processes and personalities of government whilst engaged in the practice of the law. I have sat with prime ministers, advising them on personal problems far removed from the affairs of state.

I have also seen, at close quarters, great men in charge of small countries; from them I understood the meaning of the word humility. I have also seen too the effect of power on small men, puffed up by pride and conceit. How often have I thought, in the latter cases, of Shakespeare's wonderfully apt words, 'Mere man, dressed in a little brief authority, plays such fantastic tricks before high heaven as make the angels weep'.

Yet the experience has heightened my regard for political leaders who, in democracies, bear such a daily burden on their shoulders, and whose every breath and movement is the subject of public analysis. Leading a country is no easy task. I am reminded of an old rabbinic prayer in which God is thanked 'for not making me famous'.

So many pictures flash before my eyes; sitting at a Cabinet meeting held on a tropical beach amidst palm trees and falling coconuts; being given a car, driver and escort and told to go around the country and see it all; advising on a myriad of governmental activities from oil exploration in territorial waters to the establishment of a shipping register, from the takeover by the state of a national industry in private hands to the regulation of a national bank and a national airline.

A European country asked me to help in the employment problems of their nationals in Britain, whilst an African government sought advice on a mammoth international loan they were taking. The size of the documentation their diplomats presented to me was in inverse proportion to the number of noughts in the proposed dollar loan.

My report to that government baldly stated that 'no people would ever forgive a government that mortgaged their future so heavily and so inescapably'. The loan never proceeded, apparently to the concern of some ministers and officials inclined to favour it for reasons, I suspect, far removed from the well-being of their country.

Coming from my Jewish background, immersed from childhood in the great figures of the Bible, I was vastly intrigued to find one Commonwealth government represented in London by a High Commission which included three diplomats surnamed Solomon, Hezekiah, and Jeremiah.

It is the story of Jeremiah, sadly long since returned to his eternal home, that I wish to tell – the story of the friendly consul who was mightily wronged.

The Story

It is not often realised that the right to claim diplomatic immunity is the right of the overseas government, and not of the individual whose name is on the diplomatic list. The level of immunity may be almost absolute in the case of an ambassador, more limited for those lower down the hierarchy, and non-existent for local residents taken on as staff. Governments are chary of invoking this right. It works reciprocally. It stems from diplomatic conventions, the Vienna Convention of 1964, the Brussels Convention, international agreements, and diplomatic practice. These days ambassadors are not sent abroad to lie for their country. Most of them have a vast range of genuine activities to supervise, from commerce to culture, passports to public relations.

There are a few embassies in London that have landed themselves in all manner of trouble by ignoring parking rules consistently, or planning laws provocatively. When the British press and public react strongly to this obnoxious exercise of privilege, home governments take note and emissaries suddenly find themselves posted to exercise their skills in Outer Nowhere or beyond.

The hero of this tale was very much London-based, but possessed of the cheerful creative qualities of his native land. He loved a rum punch, a lively steel band, dancing, and carnival. We met at celebrations, national day functions, and occasionally our families went out together. A manly man, macho some might say, he was particularly attentive to the opposite sex, liked, and was liked by, women.

Travelling one day on London's Underground system, he waited on the platform at Fulham Broadway for his train. Tube trains do not always keep to their timetables. He waited and waited, until the call of nature became pressing. He entered a toilet, and a few minutes later emerged under arrest; he and two older men. He was shattered. He had heard of the arbitrary behaviour of a few police officers, from complaints received from fellow nationals, but this was his first personal experience of a sad and perplexing phenomenon.

He was shattered, not only for being arrested by a plain clothes officer so suddenly, so wrongly, but also by the nature of the charge. To this manly man, to be accused of indecent behaviour with two other men was a final insult. For him – husband, father of four, a regular fellow – to be tainted with any level of homosexuality or indecency was beyond his comprehension.

It was also beyond the comprehension of his Biblical and non-Biblical colleagues. They knew what utter nonsense the charge was. They knew their man. The question was, what was to be done about it? Protest to the Foreign and Commonwealth Office? Protest to New Scotland Yard? Follow usual diplomatic channels? It was a problem. The police detective had filed his report. He had provided detail, chapter and verse. He had signed his report. To go back on it would expose him to all kinds of sanctions. He had to stand by it for the sake of his career.

The British Government dared not intervene. The executive could not be seen interfering with the criminal or judicial process. Withdrawal of a serious indictable charge required the consent of the Director of Public Prosecutions, a consent that could only be construed as a concession to diplomatic relations, flying in the face of written, signed evidence. British justice did not work that way.

Jeremiah, like his prophetic namesake, seemed to be alone, on the edge of disaster, but, again like the ancient seer, help was at hand. His own government would back him. They would not raise the issue of diplomatic immunity, which would not have cleared his name. They would back him through the courts. They would take care of their own. They knew their man.

Other strange problems arose. At the lower magistrates' court, the two men also accused wished to plead guilty. This admission could have been disastrous for our man. I asked them if they were guilty. They replied that they were not. So why admit a charge that was false? They dare not risk publicity, and the effect it would have on their families.

I came upon a new phenomenon: men claiming innocence yet prepared to plead guilty. How often, I wondered, did this happen? A perceptive psychologist was needed. Perhaps they had guilty minds, but had done nothing culpable. I spent an hour in the corridor persuading these men to defer their plea, and finally succeeded. We spent but a minute in the court and left to fight another day. The two men consulted a solicitor, who thankfully agreed to follow our lead.

I studied the police papers intently. Something was wrong. The detective said he looked out from a grille above a single toilet door, and could see, unobserved, all that was happening in another specific part of the general toilet area. He then let his pornographic mind run riot. He must have spent his nights imbibing Rabelais, de Sade and blue movies. When sexually aroused, I gather, the head of the agama lizard turns blue. Our detective's head must have shared both the colour and the moral qualities of that reptile.

I raised questions with the prosecution, who confirmed the precise details of the detective's point of observation through holes in the grille. Written confirmation – never trust telephone calls.

With this in hand, I went along to the station toilet with enquiry agent, surveyor, and photographer. We proceeded to photograph, measure, and note every inch of the toilet. We took photographs through the grille, and towards the grille from the toilet. That establishment had not been so minutely examined since the architect drew the plans and the builder constructed the erection.

When we later assembled to discuss our findings, it was obvious the detective could never have seen what he claimed he had witnessed. It was arrant nonsense, a cock-and-bull story.

The jury were sworn in. The judge explained to them their function. All was polite, formal. Prosecuting Counsel calmly outlined his case. The jury shuffled in their seats. Sexual cases were unsettling, sometimes embarrassing. They glanced at the three men in the dock. Some of the jurymen and women may already have made up their minds on hearing of such a disgusting encounter. The detective gave his evidence. He sounded convincing. A colleague confirmed some details.

'Mr Sebag Shaw', the judge turned to defending counsel. We had instructed Sebag Shaw QC and Michael Sherrard (also later Queen's

Counsel), two of the most brilliant criminal practitioners at the Bar. We had right on our side, truth on our side, but above all, evidence on our side.

What followed in the next three hours was the deadliest cross-examination I have ever heard. Lie after lie emerged from the officer, contradiction after contradiction, one untruth conceded, and explained away by another untruth. It was merciless, agonising. Were it a boxing match, the towel would have been thrown in long before. The judge watched intently, despite his elevated impartiality. The jury leaned forward, craned forward, practically out of their seats.

At the end of three hours, the main prosecution witness was totally devastated, discredited. The prosecution, the judge nodding his assent, hastily asked to withdraw the charges. The case was over, yet we, as human beings, were all diminished by the behaviour of another human being – that single police detective.

The usual things followed – costs, compensation, apology – but nothing could atone for what my friend and client had suffered. The two men, minded to plead guilty, were free, reputations untarnished, although who knew what was in their minds. The police officer stood trial for perjury and was, unbelievably, acquitted. One day our criminal justice system will take a harder, more piercing look at itself and at the unreality of much of its procedure.

And Jeremiah? He died at an early age from hypertension. Did he ever get over the experience? Did the injustice of it, the sheer moral brutality of it, ever depart from within him? Or did it fester and finally destroy him? He was a kind of martyr, who never chose martyrdom. I pay tribute to his memory.

And for what? Because a weak police officer was late back on duty, had to cover himself with his superiors, provide some explanation, so walked into a toilet notorious for immoral behaviour, grabbed two likely-looking suspects, and swept up a third in the process. Had he any idea of the consequences of his mean and thoughtless action, especially in relation to the third man, he would have done much better to admit his laziness and face the wrath of his local police Inspector. He had abused his authority and, though lucky to escape conviction, suffered the consequences. But those consequences were wider than he could have imagined.

Mere man continues to make the angels weep – and not only the angels.

Chapter VII

And a Little Child Shall Lead Them
or *Horns of a Dilemma*

Introduction

I doubt whether any cases have disturbed me more than those relating to children. I was fortunate. I had a happy childhood, two parents, grandparents, a host of uncles, aunts, and cousins. Whatever was lacking materially was more than compensated for by a warmth and richness of relationships.

It is against this personal background that I have watched with a heavy heart, sometimes indignation, often sympathy, the parade of children's cases with which I have had to deal. In a way, the law is the worst instrument to resolve these issues, yet society has so far failed to find a better one.

A host of organisations exist to help – The Children's Society, Dr. Barnados Homes, the National Society for Prevention of Cruelty to Children, Norwood Child Concern – yet if parents who brought children into the world knew their duty, and carried out their trust, there would be no need for these societies, no need for the numerous childrens' homes operated by local authorities up and down the land.

Rarely can we open a newspaper or watch the screen without some terrible report of a child abused, neglected, assaulted, murdered. Inquiries in the 1980s were set up, at Cleveland, Greenwich, Brent, into child abuse and the responsibility of local authority social services staff.

In 1992, a prosecution showed the horror of mass abuse at a Leicestershire childrens' home. Children were scarred for life. It also showed the sadistic cruelty of people placed in charge of these homes, the lack of control by the council committees concerned, and the fear and victimisation of those employed in the service who are prepared to speak up for the victims. Some of the children have been harmed more by these homes than those from which they were originally taken. It is by publicising these derelictions of duty that the press can perform a public service, and frequently does. But these reports relate to public institutions.

It is when husband and wife fall out, separate, divorce, that children so often become the innocent instruments of retribution and revenge. Wild allegations fly about in affidavits as to the unsuitability of one parent to be allowed custody or care and control (pre-Children Act 1989 terms), or even access to the children of the family. Personal secrets entrusted, one to the other, when harmony reigned, are suddenly disclosed to the world. The other party is demonised and dehumanised, adopting the practice of wartime propaganda concerning an enemy. Children are kept away from grandparents, usually as punishment for the other spouse, although the law has now moved a little to recognise grandparental rights.

A frequent problem is where a child is suddenly wafted abroad, abducted, often by one spouse sincerely believing that it is in the best interest of the child. In my career, there are faces expressing shock and sadness, as well as suffering, I can never forget. One was of an internationally celebrated barrister who walked into my office, seeking help. His face was a picture of despair, desolation, disbelief.

To his horror, this virile, dynamic man had discovered not merely that his wife, whom he so esteemed, was having an affair with another woman, but he had seen them together in his own bedroom, in his own bed.

He was shattered. In no way could he allow his children to be cared for by a mother involved in a practice he so despised. They had to be removed from her influence at once. I explained court procedure. It was not quick enough. The law's delays, its neutral niceties, its procedural quagmires, were not for him. Before anyone knew, the children disappeared, and re-appeared in a far-off country, beyond the law's or the mother's reach. Possession was indeed nine tenths of the law.

I recall too a prominent overseas lawyer who flew into London and into my office. His wife had abducted their child. Would I go to Paris and bring the child back? Legal men, in their own affairs, sometimes have simplistic approaches. I went to Paris – never a hardship – and found the child and the mother. Both were well and happy.

I heard the wife's side of the story (useful for a lawyer, yet often debilitating for his enthusiastic advocacy of his own client's cause). The mother had a case. She explained, sensibly and fully, what she had done and why. She had not really considered the blow her action represented to her husband's pride, his *amour-propre*, his local standing.

Somehow I got them together, a *modus vivendi* was reached, and the three of them respected the terms agreed, to their joint benefit. Years later, I met the daughter. She had grown into a fine young woman, seemingly unaffected by this episode. She remained close to both parents, who respected each other.

In this case the personal approach was far more effective than the gladiatorial confrontation of the law courts. All the court orders in the world – and the husband had obtained a few in his own country – would not have reconciled that family to each other.

In the meantime the law moved on. 1985 saw a Child Abduction and Custody Act and a European convention to limit the chances of successful removal of children from their home countries. But it remains a heartbreaking problem when one parent has taken a child to a country whose courts pay little attention to the rights of another parent, especially a wife.

In England we are gradually moving towards family courts, yet I wonder whether any kind of court is what we really want. The more extensive the law in family matters, the more it is a recognition of the failure of family life, just as the expanding criminal law is an acknowledgment of the failure of the moral law to govern relationships. The Ten Commandments, or Utterances, delivered on Mount Sinai were brief enough, 343 words in all. In 1992, *Stone's Justices Manual*, dealing with the work of magistrates' courts, ran to 6500 pages, whilst *Blackstone's Criminal Practice* of the same year had a mere 2889 pages. Law has become not merely an avenue to justice, a vocation, but an industry.

Over the years, I have noticed that failure of marriages often arise from cultural differences between the parties. The more a husband and wife have in common as to background, religion, language, food, values, the greater the chance of a successful union. Whilst relationships may be heaven-sent, marriage – formal, legal marriage – is a man-made institution, and a very sensible one. Its success breeds success. Its failure breeds failure.

Early in my career I came across Indian immigrants who married blonde au pair girls from Holland, Scandinavia and other parts of

Europe. Later I saw West Indians who married Africans, both black-skinned. Often these marriages foundered on basic cultural and value differences. The children became confused. Perhaps I saw only the unsuccessful liaisons. Religious differences added to personality problems. What was the religion's attitude to the rights of fathers and mothers over children, over the wife's role? A child born to a Jewish mother was Jewish, irrespective of marriage or fatherhood. In Islam, rights and status stemmed from the father. The 1950s and 1960s brought other faiths into Britain, sometimes for the first time.

There could sometimes be quite unanticipated consequences of a marital breakdown. I recall the delicate problem of a Prime Minister, not British, whose marriage had foundered, partly on personality, partly on cultural differences. How was I to deal with the matter for him without rocking the political boat?

There were children, there were houses. There were, according to the wife, other women. Her status, her standing were affected. What would the effect be on their children whom both loved, and who loved them? They asked each other, and explored, this sensible question. They were sensible people.

We met together, clients and lawyers, and hammered out a solution that lasted. The press were never involved. Marriages are lived on different levels. They decided to live together, and apart, in a way that respected their public image and private problems. A lower level of marriage, but one which, as time went on, proved workable. He remained Prime Minister, she remained his wife, and although the heart had gone out of the union, the form remained. Sometimes the form itself has a value – to protect children from hurt. But it is second best.

Bernard Shaw once asserted that most married couples live in a state of quiet desperation. I do not agree. There are many happy, loving marriages. When these occur, they are a blessing to themselves, to society, and especially to their children.

But as the rate of divorce and separation increase in Western countries, from which royal families are not immune, can we possibly estimate the ultimate effect on society of the sense of insecurity, conflict of loyalties, and disturbed values created in the children.

It is difficult enough in private relationships, but when the law, through its social welfare agencies, takes a hand, the result can sometimes prove parlous and destructive.

The Story

One of the fascinations of living and practising in London in the last few decades has been to observe the knitting together of an ethnic tapestry of many varied shades and qualities. Jains, Sikhs, Bahais, have developed their religious centres and temples. One of the largest ethnic groups has been the Hindus, from Gujarat and other parts of mother India, but coming also from East Africa, the Caribbean and the Far East, whence colonial rulers had transported them to serve as cheap, indentured labour.

Wherever they have wandered through the great Indian Diaspora, they have retained that natural religious impulse that has produced religious teachers of distinction, Mahatma Gandhi being the best known, but others of saintly quality combined with practical concern.

I have observed this particularly in some of the Swaminarayan centres in London, where voluntary service is of the essence, particularly in the fabulous (only word that does it justice) temple erected in north-west London in the mid-1990s, relying on the dedication of 1700 voluntary workers. But the story I relate concerns another Hindu sect, the Bharat Sevasran Sangh, and one of its London homes, and particularly one family it had housed.

The sect has the highest aims: to help the distressed, to foster the spiritual, cultural and ancient heritage of India, and to promote tolerance among followers of different faiths. Their inspiration was an acharya, a master, born in 1896. He founded the brotherhood in 1916 and died in 1941. He taught that 'The essence of religion lies in its practice and realisation'. In pursuit of this ideal, the sect had set up educational centres throughout the world, as well as homes in which their adherents could live until finding more suitable accommodation.

One such home was in west London, a large house in which dwelt several families. The family I was concerned with lived in the basement with their three young daughters. The oldest, a seven-year-old, had lived much of her life abroad with an elderly grandmother, as happens in many immigrant families, in fact happened to my own mother.

The child had hurt herself, and was referred by her school to a hospital. Suddenly the harmless devout parents received a letter from the social services department of a London borough stating that the child was not to be returned home, that the council would take parental control of the child, a Place of Safety Order (renamed subsequently as an Emergency Protection Order) would be sought from the courts authorising the council to keep the child in its custody, and a Care Order was to be applied for so that the child would be kept in one of the council's homes, away from parents, friends, sisters, neighbours. Thus, came the bald announcement in an official-looking letter.

The parents were devastated. They had little money. Life was a struggle. The father, 32 years old, worked on London's telephone exchange system. He was trying to improve himself and earn more. Both had been but a short time in the country. They were scared of authority and official-looking letters. They sought help. They were sent to me. I saw them. They were confused, upset, uncomprehending. We activated the legal aid system, which at least could cover basic costs, and began to investigate.

It was clear that social services had panicked. The press and TV had highlighted a major scandal of a child named Maria Caldwell, who had died as a result of parental brutality unperceived by social services. If Maria had been removed in time, she might have survived. Perhaps, social welfare officers reasoned, the Indian child could be another Maria. Her few bruises might be the start of a parental onslaught which they could quickly bring to an end. It was a dilemma, as it always is for social service departments – to act or not to act, to be precipitate and be blamed, or procrastinate and be blamed. It was not easy – a no-win situation.

I had previously sat in on social services case studies, where officers from different sections of a local authority discussed a single case in depth. I had observed officers who were compassionate yet professional, those who merely went through the motions of a job, perhaps inured to the dramatic reality of each case by the volume of referrals they had to contend with, and others who seemed to me to be disturbed themselves, working out their own problems through the case in hand.

But for our seven-year-old Indian child a Place of Safety Order had been made, as well as an interim Care Order, in the absence of any legal representation on behalf of the child or the parents. The council thus had legal backing for their action. But the council were deficient. They had made no real study of the family. They had behaved with arrogance.

I went to the parents' house, interviewed them, other residents, the Swami in charge, the child's doctor. The council had spoken to none of them. They had seen some bruises on a sickly-looking child, bruises on the knees and elbows, as well as ear problems, had taken fright, rushed the child into a council centre, and hurried along to the court for legal backing.

I was furious. A child had been removed from her parents – a sad and traumatic event whatever the facts – with no understanding of the history, background, culture, or even an alternative explanation of the injuries. As a child myself, I was continually full of bruises. My own children were always getting bruised. It happens to any lively active child, climbing trees, falling down in the school playground, bumping into furniture, playing games.

I was constantly in hospital having dressings applied to bruised knees following over-enthusiastic football matches on gravel or tarmacked surfaces. Should I have been removed from my home, made the subject of a court order? Should the same have happened to my own children? Social services should have done their job and investigated this case properly, before so arbitrarily breaking up a family. They would have discovered facts of crucial relevance.

They would have found out that the child had been born prematurely, weighing 3lb 6oz at birth, had suffered from a local illness which she was gradually overcoming in England, and had not lived with her parents during her first few years until her father had earned enough money to bring her to England.

They would have discovered that the parents were kindness itself, as all neighbours confirmed; that neighbours even entrusted their own children to the care of the parents; that the eldest daughter was just establishing her relationship with the parents after her sojourn abroad; that the child and her two younger sisters were closely attached; that other families in the home saw the child daily; that there had never been any record of violence by the parents; and that the Swami, the religious leader, had known the parents for six years and was only too happy to have them in the house.

They would have learned that the child's doctor had been shocked not to have been consulted by them, when he knew all about the child's problems, as the child had stated clearly she had been injured in the school playground. And if the parents were considered to be a danger to the one child, was it not possible that they were also a danger to the two younger children, who were never removed from the home?

I obtained all the evidence the council should have discovered: independent medical and social welfare evidence, and evidence about the problems at school. Large sums of public money were thus spent on both sides of the issue, expenses which need never have been incurred.

However, there was a court order and the child was still in a council home. She could not eat the food. She was used to the Indian food her parents provided. Her parents brought her clothes. Visitors noted that other children were wearing them. A nurse, friend of the parents, observed that the child had suffered bruising whilst living in the home. The story was appalling.

I went back to the court to have the interim Care Order discharged, so that the child could be returned home. The court would not listen. It needed time to hear all the facts. Its lists were full. Come back next month.

I returned next month. One of the magistrates suddenly discovered she had discussed the case with a council officer and thereby disqualified herself from sitting in judgment. Another magistrate could not be found. Come back next month.

It was scandalous. Meanwhile, a child was separated from her parents. The father, who had worked so hard to save money to bring his child to join him, had to visit her in a council home, while the court looked in its diary for a convenient date to hear the case.

I exploded, went straight to the High Court, and requested that the magistrates be directed to find a convenient date. The judge agreed and told the magistrates to re-arrange their lists and hear the case. They still prevaricated.

Eventually they heard the evidence they should have heard originally, and made the order they should have made in the first place, namely to leave the child at home, but if social services were worried, to let them play some supervisory role, to keep an eye on things, in case anything untoward was happening.

The child returned home immediately. She had been kept apart from her parents for eight months; a separation which made adjustment more difficult, which would always be somewhere in the back of the child's mind, might affect her future relationships, her own sense of security. Who really knows what goes on, consciously or unconsciously, in the inner mind, the soul, of a young impressionable child.

In the next three months, social services, originally so concerned that they had to keep the child in their control every day, managed to visit the family but twice, and then gave up altogether. The family obtained a larger flat, moved in, and lived a normal family life – except for the shadow of the courts, the implied accusations, and the enforced separation.

I have not the slightest doubt that there are cases in which children, for their own safety, should be removed from parents. It requires a great deal of skill and knowledge to decide when to act. Recent evidence has uncovered a wider range of child abuse than was previously thought to exist. It may be that council officers will always live on the horns of a dilemma.

One can only be saddened by a society in which defenceless children are abused, not merely by parents or step-parents, but also by the very people in charge of children's homes who are supposed to be their protectors. 'Even as you do unto these little ones, so you do unto me.' The words of Jesus could become the words of society itself, for by injuring children we are damaging the future fabric and health of the country.

And what of our court system? It is at least encouraging to note that the Children Act 1989 which radically changed previous Children and Young People Acts, even allowing a child to be assessed while remaining in the family home, also contains a requirement for the court to set down a timetable in each case and generally take control of proceedings to cut down on delay.

It is a pious hope. Inevitable problems have arisen from the new Act. Much more to the point would be to look at an entirely new approach. Why must we always think along traditional court procedural lines? Why cannot the magistrates and experts and lawyers all sit down together and be part of a case study? Out of it, without 'my Lords' and 'your Worships', without the printed forms *guardian ad litems* etc., perhaps truth will emerge, solutions will emerge, understanding will emerge.

Perhaps this is heresy, blasphemy, and even worse, in the eyes of the profession, but the rule of law should not mean the rule of lawyers. Until we find a more practical and less legalistic path, the question of quick, fair and sensitive treatment of the perceived problems between parents and children will not be effectively tackled.

The celebrated Swami who founded the Indian sect which had given hospitality to the family, would have looked at the morality beneath the surface of the law, the purpose of life, and the purpose of law. He saw our present age as one of 'universal awakening, re-adjustment and emancipation'. How, I wonder, would he have regarded the case of the seven-year-old daughter of two of his adherents? Probably with greater self-discipline and greater patience than I had shown. Certainly with a larger sympathy and deeper understanding for the frailty of our human kind, including the frailty of social service officers and magistrates trying to do what they saw as their duty, irrespective of the consequences.

Chapter VIII

King Arthur

or *Whatever Happened to Mrs McKay?*

Introduction

As 1969 merged into 1970 I was travelling down the west coast of Trinidad, past the great oil refinery of Pointe-à-Pierre, towards the townships of Couva and California, through Caroni's mangrove swamps with their spectacular flights of scarlet ibis and white egrets, on to San Fernando, the country's second largest town. To the south lay rich oil fields and the famous asphalt lake. Little did I know that on my return to the winter chills of England I would be faced with a case of huge proportions, linked to a family emanating from that very Couva region I had just left.

The case of the Hosein brothers, of the abduction of Mrs Muriel McKay, was, at the time, the largest in British criminal history. It was the first kidnapping case ever in Britain. It has been the subject of films on television, of many books (the best by William Cowper) and of legal and evidential analysis. Yet because of our unsatisfactory criminal procedure, the most important point in the whole bizarre episode was never once mentioned in court.

The fact that the elder of the two brothers, Arthur, appeared in court wearing a different suit daily, and a dinner jacket on the last day, elicited no comment, possibly because judge and counsel were equally strangely attired. To this day, I ask myself how it was possible to conduct a case, week after week, the centre of the media's attention, without a word about a crucial element in the whole sad story.

England is entitled to pride itself on its rule of law, judicial review, honest administration, and gifted judiciary, its great gift to the world of the common law, but criminal procedure is not her crowning glory. The 1990s saw a flock of past convictions overturned as unsafe, while innocents who had lingered for years in prison were released. To anyone who does not have a sense of shame about this appalling situation I would recommend the reading of a startling book by journalist David Rose entitled *In the Name of the Law – The Collapse of Criminal Justice* (Vintage).

The whole criminal system needs a critical eye, not merely by Royal Commissions. The basis of the confrontational system, from police station and magistrates' court to the House of Lords appeal jurisdiction, should be crisply assessed, without fear, favour, nostalgia, or pride. There are judges, lawyers, and non-lawyers, with both knowledge and the courage to do so.

Two brothers, Arthur and Nizamodeen Hosein, were accused of kidnapping and murdering Mrs McKay. They pleaded not guilty. They were both found guilty. Mrs McKay was never found. No one to this day knows what happened to her. What we do know is what happened for weeks on end in Number One Court at the Old Bailey, where the presiding judge was Sir Sebag Shaw, well-known to me from many other encounters. Judge and jury, the packed gallery, and the myriad of newspaper, radio, and television journalists heard as strange a story as could be envisaged by any imaginative novelist.

The Story

For generations, intrepid men and women had journeyed from Britain to the furthest corners of the globe, creating an empire of unparalleled size, which later evolved into a commonwealth of nations. From the end of the Second World War, a procedure of journeying in reverse operated. People from many lands, in and out of the Commonwealth, have increasingly sought to settle in the United Kingdom.

By 1969 there had come from Trinidad Arthur Hosein, and, much later, his younger brother Nizam. From West Germany had come Arthur's wife, Maria. From Australia had come Alick and Muriel McKay. All were thrown together as actors in a single drama, at first played out in the suburbs and villages of southern England, later in the theatre of an English criminal court.

Arthur had prospered as a tailor and had bought a house and farm in Stocking Pelham, a small Hertfordshire village near Bishops Stortford, 30 miles north of London. He had ambitions as a potential country squire. He and his German wife already had two young children.

I visited the brothers Hosein in prison, Arthur clearly the dominant force. I was asked to represent them, but acted solely for Nizamodeen. Nizam, very much the younger brother, did what he was told, 'a stranger in a strange land', as his presence in England was later described.

Arthur was of medium height, dark complexion, rich, wavy, black hair undulating back thickly over his head above a similarly fertile but carefully-tended moustache. His eyes were piercing, large, and black. He moved compactly, like a panther.

Nizam was pale, slightly built, resembled his brother in no single particular, would be inconspicuous in a room, was obviously worried, but by no means a simpleton. Arthur's wife impressed me as lively, sturdy, outgoing, remarkably calm and steady in the face of hundreds of policemen who later combed her home and farm searching for the missing Mrs McKay. Her children were quite small, exceptionally friendly. I often played with them on my visits to the farm. They were fortunately unaware of the grim game being played out by the adults in their lives.

The father of the two accused was a Muslim lay preacher, a genuine and courteous man. He seemed totally at a loss at what was happening to his sons. He had come over, or 'up', as the expression has it, from the Caribbean on hearing of the plight of Arthur and Nizam, although there was nothing he could do or say to help them. He had brought a large *Koran* with him. Each word or phrase of the Suras, or chapters, had, at the foot of its page, long explanations and commentaries. He used to sit and explain them to me, just as my rabbis did with the words of the *Torah*, the first five books of the Bible. The two faiths have much in common.

Mr and Mrs McKay lived in an elegant Wimbledon home. He travelled daily to his important post as deputy chairman of a famous Sunday newspaper, while she remained at home. It was from that home that she mysteriously disappeared.

An operations room had been set up in the local Wimbledon Police Station, not far from the famous tennis centre. From this room, like the nerve-centre of a war campaign, went out orders which, it was hoped, would lead to the arrest of the kidnappers. Eventually Arthur and Nizam were arrested and charged.

Each week after their arrest the prisoners were brought before the local magistrates' court, as procedure then dictated, and the hearing adjourned endlessly while prosecution lawyers, presumably working overtime, prepared the enormous volume of statements to be supplied to the court and to the defence.

After the minute-long weekly court hearing, during which Arthur frequently exploded with threats and accusations, while Nizam remained perpetually mute, I often sat talking at police headquarters to Chief Superintendent Smith, a tough-talking Lancastrian, and his more urbane Chief Inspector, John Minors. These two had been in day-to-day charge of a massive operation involving hundreds of uniformed police and detectives of the Criminal Investigation Department.

When Mrs McKay disappeared from her home, after evidence of a fight, and subsequent calls for ransom payment were received there by her husband, the police realised they were faced with a case of kidnapping.

No police force in the country had ever dealt with a kidnapping case before. Advice was sought from Australia, the United States, clairvoyants; from anyone who could throw light on the mystery. For weeks thereafter the police were teased and taunted, played with, sent on false errands and wild goose-chases, by 18 long telephone calls from the kidnappers, contemptuous of police inability even to begin to trace a single clue.

The content of these calls is illuminating. I quote some extracts:

'This is Mafia group three. We are from American Mafia number three. We have your wife.' (The Mafia had nothing to do with the matter).

'We have your wife. It will cost you £1 million to get her back. We tried to get Rupert Murdoch's wife, we couldn't get her, so we took yours instead.' (Rupert Murdoch was Alick McKay's immediate boss.)

'Muriel is very nice, very co-operate, well taken care of.' (Imagine her husband's feelings.)

'If you don't co-operative, you're to be blamed for not seeing your wife again.'

'Mr McKay, this is not one person, group, this is in a worldwide international. I run this branch in England. We have never murdered anyone, as yet, but there will always be a first time.' (Mr McKay and his son were asking for proof that Mrs McKay was still alive, and were not arguing with the kidnapper.)

There followed an explanation of the organisation of the gang:

'This is a meeting I'm on my way to. Well, first our business is being handled by the intellectuals, the heads. Now there is a meeting of the semi-intellectuals, to be passed on to the third party, the ruffians. This meeting is in consideration with your mum, what time she be executed, whether she should be executed and what time you see. I'm going to plead for your mum. I'm fond of your mum because she reminds me of my mum you see.'

The caller, talking to Mrs McKay's son in these terms, then started to be concerned about his own safety:

'If they (the organisation) caught me here now, I shall be executed. I'm thinking of resigning. My life is in danger as well. I'm being watched in every footstep I make. I'm not trusted any more. I'm being threatened and I got to do what they say.'

In the end, the arrest of the two brothers came about more by chance than by planning. The Chief Superintendent had tried to question the two, without success. The most he ever got was a cry from Nizam, 'I wish I were dead'. Smith shook his head as he complained to me, 'Those men have pulled a shutter down on their minds'. Not a glimmer of an admission emerged from all his questioning.

And, of course, there was no body. He would have to prove that Mrs McKay was dead; had actually been taken by these two unresponsive men in his custody. All kinds of rumours spread as to what had happened to Mrs McKay, none of which convinced me.

At one stage of our tortuous procedure, I asked the prosecution to let me have all the statements they had taken which they did not intend to produce in evidence. There had been a public appeal for knowledge of the whereabouts of Mrs McKay, and there had been a considerable response.

There were over a thousand statements. I read them all. Few helped. Many described how they had seen Mrs McKay walking about in different parts of Britain long after she had disappeared. An eminent university professor had submitted a detailed theory as to what had happened to the missing lady. All manner of people had let their imaginations run riot.

Eventually we came to trial. The court had been wired to play recorded telephone messages. It was proposed for the first time in our courts to produce evidence of voice prints. They were supposed to be as infallible as fingerprints. They had been the subject of Solzhenitsyn's *The First Circle*, and utilised by American and Soviet espionage agents. They had never been used as evidence in a British court. It was a blow to the prosecution when the judge said he would not accept that kind of evidence.

But evidence galore there was: paper, ink, indentations on blank sheets beneath other sheets on which ransom demands had been written, handwriting, fingerprints, knowledge of English, rope, meat cleavers, motor vehicles, telephone calls, paper flowers – all the many exhibits that accumulated on the table in the well of the court.

One amusing incident involved a famous expert in the witness box who confirmed that certain handwriting was that of Nizam. John Minors sitting nearby nudged me, 'What is he talking about? That is my writing.' The expert's face fell when told of his mistake. This confirmed my reservations about experts in a witness box, to whom judges defer quite excessively.

There was a bizarre quality about the phone calls. They spoke of special spots where the ransom money was to be dropped, in suitcases. They spoke of the groups in their organisation: the intellectuals, the assassins. Today the calls would have been traced in a flash – not then.

Police efforts at concealment were farcical. Sergeants crawled on their stomachs across fields. John Minors hid in a car boot. The police were baffled, though in constant touch by phone with the kidnappers.

An amusing incident related to two cases full of ransom money left on a Bishops Stortford pavement. Police were hidden all around, waiting to pounce on those collecting the cases. Some public-spirited citizen, however, noticed the cases and arranged for the local police to remove them. The hidden police, hoping to get vital evidence, were furious. Another plan that went awry. However, the registration number of a Volvo car, suspiciously active in the area, had been observed. It led directly to Arthur's farm.

The cumulative prosecution evidence was overwhelming, despite occasional problems with expert witnesses. There was a potential conflict of interest between the brothers, which is why I represented Nizam only. Arthur, eager to be centre-stage, went into the witness box, occasionally correcting both judge and counsel on their accuracy. If he was conscious of his behaviour as a witness then he was arrogant. If not, then it threw much light on his mental condition.

He mentioned a dramatic meeting at the farm in the middle of the night. He was upstairs in bed and a group of mysterious people were downstairs with Nizam. He overheard the people below mention the name of the late, unlamented newspaper proprietor Robert Maxwell. How was Arthur's mind working? He knew Maxwell and Rupert Murdoch had been in conflict. It was headline news in the media. In fact Mr and Mrs McKay had had, in that fateful week of her disappearance, the use of Rupert Murdoch's Rolls-Royce. It was widely believed that Muriel McKay was, as a result, snatched mistakenly for Mrs Murdoch; a view confirmed by the telephone callers.

Within hours of his name having been mentioned in court, a barrister rose and said on behalf of Robert Maxwell that his client had nothing to do with the affair. Surprisingly, that statement was not recorded in the transcript of the trial. It was yet another bizarre episode in an increasingly strange case.

Eventually the jury retired, after a summing-up described later by the Court of Appeal as impeccable. Both men were found guilty of all charges – murder, kidnapping, blackmail.

Arthur, from the dock, exploded, and fulminated against the judge with all manner of accusations. Nizam accepted the verdict silently, and received a lesser prison sentence than his brother.

What did happen to Mrs McKay? No one knows. The brothers are silent, despite large cash offers for their story from the press. She probably died early in the affair from shock, or from being deprived of pills on which she depended.

What happened to the brothers? Nizam was released after serving his twelve years with remission. What had never been disclosed to the court was Arthur's mental history. He had been in a mental home, was later discharged from the army because of his mental condition, and, after the case, was much later transferred from an ordinary prison to a prison mental institution.

The strange working of a damaged mind was at the heart of the terrible wrong done to Mrs McKay and her courageous but afflicted family. Yet not a word was said about it throughout the trial. Are we still proud of our criminal justice system, which can spend days on evidence as to handwriting and telephone calls and ignore completely the most fundamental element in the whole wretched affair?

What happened to Arthur's wife and children I do not know. It is believed she returned to Germany. Alick McKay continued to grieve for his lost wife, so suddenly and so cruelly taken from him. Chief Superintendent Smith died a few years later. John Minors retired. The handwriting expert went on giving expert evidence for many years. The judge passed away, full of honour and distinction.

As for me, I had a sudden urge early on in the case to play the detective, even though I employed two sets of enquiry agents. One day I scoured the fields and barns and byways of south Hertfordshire. If I could only have found Mrs McKay, that would have been an end of the case.

Naturally I did not find her. I hope, for the sake of her family, someone some day will state what happened to her. That will bring a certain amount of peace, not only to her relatives, but also to those who had committed such an appalling crime, staining not only society, but their very own souls.

Chapter IX

We Always Prosecute
or *The Shoplifter*

Introduction

Amidst the wealth of literature which I have inherited from the past – Hebrew, Yiddish, Ladino, Biblical, Talmud, Commentaries, Nobel-prize winners from Agnon to Singer, story-tellers from Shalom Aleichem to modern exponents of the Anglo-Jewish and American-Jewish literary scene – there is one perennial strand, that of Jewish humour, which is probably best known to the non-Jewish world.

It has produced famous comedians and comics, as well as filling volume after volume of droll stories – a safety valve for the tension of a frequently embattled people.

Once embarked on telling these tales, one can pass the night away in smiles and laughter, without repeating a single story. One concerns the children of Israel gathered at the foot of Mount Sinai awaiting news of the Commandments, laws, and divine words, to be issued from on high. Someone suddenly rushes over to the eagerly-awaiting tribes exclaiming, 'I have good news and bad news for you'. The people pressed him for information. 'Well', he replied, 'the good news is that we've managed to keep them down to ten. The bad news is that number seven (no adultery) is still in.'

Another 'still in' was number eight, 'Thou shalt not steal' – simple, clear, concise, bare, unqualified. It was morally wrong, divinely decreed as culpable, to take something which belonged to another. A clear injunction, as relevant in the moral chaos of today as in ancient times.

Our law has broadened out the simple concept of theft to include burglary, robbery, forgery, embezzlement – all assaults on the property of another. The basic moral law was given legal flesh in the 1968 Theft Act and reflected further in legislation and judicial decisions.

For a long time I have been concerned with the defence of people accused of shoplifting, and have frequently defended them in the magistrates' court. When opting for trial in a higher court, before a jury, I have had to instruct a barrister, although the Courts and Legal Services Act 1991 has been a help more recently. That is still the restrictive nature of our legal system. We won many cases. I used to quip that we only defended innocent people. There was some truth in that, as the professional criminal rarely sought my help.

Yet each case was a potential tragedy, irrespective of the value of the article taken. For an ordinary individual, a professional man or woman, a student, a publicly-known figure, to be hoisted into the dock on a shoplifting or theft charge was demeaning, often shattering. The charge itself, apart from the result, affected careers, promotion, relationships, self-esteem, occasionally life itself. Prominent, highly-respected television personality Lady Isobel Barnett died not long after admitting to a series of shop thefts.

The consequences of a theft charge were far greater than the monetary value of the article, or the severity of the sentence. For that reason, I have always advocated the retention of the right to a jury trial for the accused. A lifetime's career could be at stake, and should not be sacrificed to the administrative convenience of the courts. Courts exist for the benefit of the people, not the other way round – something the whole judicial system should ever bear in mind.

Whilst not excusing theft, one can understand the phenomenon in past centuries, when dire poverty was endemic. The penalty in those days was death, or transportation to the far colonies. Yet today, in a welfare state, where no one need starve, where all manner of financial benefits are available, it is remarkable that theft, shoplifting especially, has become an epidemic.

The tenth Commandment, 'Thou shalt not covet', reflecting intention, greed, the internal mental and emotional mechanism leading to the physical act, is also ignored and disregarded. Our public relations and advertising industry are geared to the converse proposition – 'Thou shalt covet'. Covetousness, among the morally weak, poor, and rich alike, leads frequently to theft.

There is barely a magistrate who cannot tell of the weekly saga of men and women appearing before them in these sad cases: defendants ranging from public figures to tramps, potentates and princes possessed of untold wealth, to the housewife scrimping to make ends meet. The same excuses roll out, 'I didn't know', 'I didn't mean to', 'I didn't intend to', 'I don't know what came over me', 'I was going to return it', 'I didn't know I had it'. Even where these were genuine responses, the pervasiveness of the crime created a certain cynicism in branches of the law connected with prosecution and punishment.

Shops, especially the great department stores, suffer enormously. They set aside a balance sheet figure annually for estimated loss by theft. They employ detectives, security men, security methods. They announce to their customers boldly and clearly, 'We always prosecute'. They treat all shoplifters alike. This is a crude approach, for not all who steal are alike, or act out of the same motives.

Were I to categorise the different types of shoplifters I would list them as the compulsive, the cry for help, the challenger, the innocent, and the professional. What follows are illustrations of types I have come across over the years.

The Story

The Compulsive
I recall a respectable accountant; family man, good job, children, his own house. He sat in my office, head between his hands, tears in his eyes. All he had worked for was at risk. He could not rid himself of a fatal addiction – gambling. He had gambled away a fortune, enough to have provided for him and his family for life. Only it was not his money. It was his employers. It is a disease, comparable to the affliction of the compulsive alcoholic or drug-taker.

Gambling, drugs, eating, not eating – all can become addictions, compulsions. Add shoplifting to the list. Where is the shoplifting gene or chromosome? Is there a DNA strand marked shoplifting? Prison is no solution, punishment no deterrence. There is a case in point.

Selfridges is undoubtedly one of the great shops of London. It stands like some imposing Greek temple in Oxford Street, W1. It is indeed a kind of temple, to the sacred trinity of producer, consumer, and free market.

A security officer watched the disappearance of a small tin of metal polish into the bag of a male shopper, where it remained until the man left the store. The officer approached him as he stood on the pavement. Traffic roared by. Anonymous pedestrians swirled past them. Politely the security man asked about the tin. They found it in the bag. 'Sorry.'

They returned to the managers office. The police were called. 'We always prosecute.' Not a bad lapse, thought the police. Still, it had to be dealt with. Formalities were concluded.

The shopper was leaving, minus his tin of polish. Suddenly an intuitive wave enveloped the officer. What is intuition? An aggregation of intelligence, reason and experience, clicking away silently in the subconscious? Whatever it is, the policeman had it. He decided to accompany the shopper home. He had reason to suspect: better, intuition to suspect.

They walked together, the officer not knowing what he would find, whether he was wasting his time. The metal polisher had no objection.

Into his home they went. The officer's mouth dropped open, his eyes glazed over. The modest apartment was a veritable treasure trove, an Aladdin's cave. It was a private department store, an art gallery, several art galleries, silver shining brightly, a world of immense wealth.

Every item, hundreds upon hundreds, had been stolen. Their value was assessed at hundreds of thousands of pounds. No excuses were offered. The Selfridges shopper had taken them all. Never a problem. He had walked into art galleries, taken paintings off the wall, and walked out. Never a problem, never challenged.

The police filled cars, vans, lorries, spread out the articles on long tables in room after room at their headquarters.

I walked along slowly, inspecting the glittering display, shaking my head. The police had the problem of finding owners. Notices were placed in newspapers, inviting inspection. The assembled loot was displayed prominently on television. Not all owners responded.

Our client was a compulsive shoplifter. He needed treatment, not prison. He was sent to prison. He had gained nothing financially from his activities. He had sold nothing. Prison never deterred one gripped by a compulsion.

In prison he found an outlet for his energy. He became an accomplished painter. His works were exhibited. One had a pride of place in our office. Eventually he was released. And eventually we received another telephone call. Another prosecution, another collection of exhibits, another prison sentence. So it went on. And so it would go on.

Glancing at the morning paper as 1993 began, and an identical case erupted in the media in 1997, I read that a 79-year-old widow hoarded 6941 items worth £60,000 during a 17-year shoplifting spree: 799 blouses, 169 handbags, 236 pairs of gloves, etc. A police officer said, 'She had never been in trouble before. A grey-haired little old lady, everybody's idea of a typical granny. I think she has a medical problem, caused through loneliness'. The officer was on the right track.

One day a solution will be found. The law alone is not enough. For compulsive shoplifters the law must find allies in the world of medicine, psychology; new forms of therapy. Perhaps a 'Shoplifters Anonymous'. Maybe it already exists, and our metal-polishing painter has found the kind of support he so desperately needed.

The Cry for Help

I really do not know if this is a true category. Psychiatrists feel it is. Those experts we employed in defence of the accused claimed that certain shoplifters, usually women in some kind of turmoil often relating to their family, unconsciously stole items to draw attention to themselves and their needs. It may be so. I am not entirely convinced. However, psychiatrists are learned men.

I recall one such woman, of Austrian origin, married to a Nigerian. Her black-skinned son could not easily adjust to his mixed parentage. She was a gentle person, law-abiding, uncomplaining. There were family tensions. She took a dose of cough mixture, of potent quality. The label on the bottle warned imbibers not to drive motor vehicles after a dose, as they might become drowsy. Later that day she emerged from a shop with a few items, undeclared to the cashier, never paid for.

The defence was twofold. Our client had a deep personal problem she could not openly express. She wanted help. This was her way of seeking help. Secondly, the cough mixture affected the clarity of her brain. She was like a semi-drunk, unaware of what she was doing.

The jury looked at this demure, fair-haired, harmless lady, listened to her sad tale of personal woe, and acquitted her. Which of the two lines of defence influenced them I do not know.

Brent Cross is a celebrated shopping centre in one of London's northern suburbs. Anything can be purchased there. Groups of women meet there for tea, shopping, and mutual sympathy. It became a social centre. Men also patronised the scores of shops, spread about on floor upon floor under one all-embracing roof. In the centre a fountain twinkled. Shoppers relaxed. Cafés galore dispensed coffee, cream cakes, and strudel.

One man in particular had made many visits. As these visits progressed, he gradually assembled at his home enough sheets of hardboard, plywood, tools, and the like, to set up his own do-it-yourself establishment. He never paid for a single item. These were not small articles. They could not be concealed. But no one stopped him. Stealing was easy, so it seemed.

I found myself dealing with two cases for him: one of theft, the other of divorce. Pointless theft seemed to be his reaction to enormous tensions at home. His young adult children were ashamed of him. His wife could not understand him. He became ashamed of himself.

Gradually the two cases merged. A lawyer also has to deal with the 'whole man' – holistic law. I spent hours with the family. Slowly the wife began to understand the crisis which afflicted her husband. The children, too, began to feel sorry for him. He had been a good father. Outside expert help was sought. What could have been a disaster instead highlighted their mutual need, as well as mutual problems. The divorce case was dropped.

In court, the family background and support influenced the sentence. All items were returned to the store, which had suffered from a gradually diminishing stock. They were, in fact, overjoyed that a large financial loss never actually materialised.

I felt satisfaction in playing some role in saving a marriage. Most solicitors do. Maybe the accumulation of building materials in his home had indeed represented a cry for help; a call for understanding and respect. I do not know, but, if it had, then truly it received its reward.

The Challenger

George Bernard Shaw stated that had he not been a dramatist, he would have liked to have been a lawyer. He also asserted in one of his typically sweeping generalisations:

'Civilisation is at present an imposture: we are a crowd of savages on whom a code of makeshift regulations is forced by penalties for breaking them.'

This 'crowd of savages' reminded me of my early years. Children are not born law-abiding. They have to learn by example and precept, by punishment and encouragement. Until they learn, they are always challenging authority. With most, the challenging notion eventually wears off in adulthood. With some it remains for life.

I recall, as a child, the constant pattern of bands of eight- and nine-year-olds, roaming the streets of east London. Groups used to enter a shop selling sweets and chocolates – a penny a bag or less in those inflationless days – and ask the owner, usually a woman, for a pennyworth of sweets from a jar high up on the furthest, topmost shelf. A ladder was required. She climbed up. While her back was turned, a frantic raid took place on the most accessible low-lying confectionery. Her stock regularly diminished as a result of the untamed rapaciousness of such rascally customers.

The children rarely saw any moral deficiency in their acts. It was a lark, fun, a challenge. They grew out of it. When caught, they were at the end of no prosecution, rather a firm clout on an appropriate part of the anatomy. Gradually they learned.

This scene of challenging persists, inevitably, among teenagers. Often it finds expression in the physical exertion, climbing, sailing, and acquiring skills of the Duke of Edinburgh's Award Scheme. Sometimes it is exhibited in the antics of college 'rag' weeks. One youngster removed from a shop a plastic figure advertising a charity. He was prosecuted. His father, then Governor of an overseas dependency, rushed to London. Eventually we managed to sort out the problem.

More difficult was the case of a couple of high-spirited college students who removed from a shop parts of its decorative furniture, including large pot plants. The shop prosecuted. The young men were extremely fortunate, for the future of their careers, to have been acquitted. They were high-spirited, could not see the harm, had no 'intention of permanently depriving the owner of his property', as the wording has it, but still it was idiotic behaviour. The lesson was salutary. They were scared to their bones by the formality of a court appearance, and the uncertainty of the result. They developed into responsible members of society.

Challengers do mischief for the fun of it; rarely for their own personal benefit. Consequences can often be more than they bargain for. It is our difficult task to teach basic rules of behaviour –

morality enshrined in law, not Shaw's contemptuous reference to a code of makeshift regulations – that have to be observed if any form of decent, civilised society is to survive. It is also our task to teach by example. There will always be the challengers – young men and women of spirit – and their adventurousness needs to be understood and channelled into constructive paths.

The Innocent

The innocent are not always found innocent. The guilty are not always found guilty. That is the problem of our system, of any system. So much is subjective, so much circumstantial. So much depends on the efficiency and the personality of the lawyers, the judges, and the juries, sometimes on prejudice, sometimes on minds made up too speedily.

Years ago, I recall an incident in the Court of Criminal Appeal. The barrister rose, 'My Lord, this is an appeal against sentence in a case where the appellant was found guilty of throwing ammonia in the eyes of a colleague'. Before he could proceed he was interrupted by the stern, unbending Lord Chief Justice, who barked, 'Need anything further be said?' Try as he could, counsel could make no further impression. A mind had been closed to further argument. Maybe Lord Goddard was right.

That rarely happens today. The judges sit quietly and listen. We are so conscious now of rights, of protection for the accused, of efforts to prevent intimidation, forced confessions. We have the Police and Criminal Evidence Act that lays down the law to the police as well as the accused, protecting the latter especially. Occasionally we lean so far backwards as to make the job of the police, our frontline in the protection of society, more difficult than it need be.

Occasionally too, one comes across a shoplifting case, brought under the undeviating rule, 'We always prosecute', whereby an obviously innocent person is dragged into court – an inexcusable process. Such was the case of Mrs G., a mild, gentle woman in her eighties. She had a benign, bewildered face under grey hair adorned by an old-fashioned hat. She walked slowly, moved slowly. I had not seen her before her appearance in court.

I was in court on that day helping all and sundry under the Duty Solicitors Scheme, whereby solicitors attended to assist unrepresented defendants. It remains a valuable scheme. I had played some part in setting it up in the local magistrates' court.

Mrs G. asked me to help her. She had been charged with theft – stealing some bread and rolls to the value of about £2. She had never been in a court in her life. She had no idea what was going on; totally bewildered.

I managed to get some inkling of the story from her, and from others. There had been a terrible storm. A tree had come down damaging her home. She was overwhelmed by the event, profoundly worried about her future. She had walked to a nearby baker's shop, part of a chain, picked up some bread, got out some money to pay, and, with her mind preoccupied, walked past the cashier into the street, where she stood looking about her.

The manager hurried after her from the shop. He told her she had taken the bread without paying. She showed him the money, still in her hand. She explained how worried she was about her home. He was not impressed at all. 'We always prosecute.' So poor Mrs G. sat there in court while the manager, thick-set, with serious white face, gave his version.

It took a lot of restraint to cross-examine this shameful individual with the courtesy I believed is always due to witnesses. Somehow I managed it, but my contempt must have shown through.

The little old lady told her story slowly, as she did everything. She really couldn't understand why she was in this strange building, with three people sitting higher than the rest listening to her. What was it all about? She left the witness box and resumed her seat, probably more concerned about her uncertain future in a badly damaged home. Old people worry deeply about their homes. They desperately need security.

Fortunately the case was dismissed. Suddenly, as it dawned on her what had been happening, her drawn face expanded into a wide, beaming smile. She rose, climbed slowly up to the magistrates, shook each of them by the hand, exclaiming, 'God bless you, God bless you'. It was the first time I had seen a bench of magistrates smile communally and blush. It did them credit. I was proud of them, and so, I hoped, would be their great protector, the Lord High Chancellor of England.

The Professional
At the other end of the spectrum from innocent Mrs G. is the professional who steals as a business. He, or she, is a discriminating

person. Bread, plywood, cotton goods are out. For him it is silver, jewellery, works of art, anything he can dispose of to characters known in the trade as 'fences', and in the courts as 'receivers'. Without the latter, the professional shoplifter's business would rapidly decline.

I came across few professional shoplifters in my career. Those few I met knew the law only too well. They had heard it expounded so frequently. They knew the Theft Act, 1968, definition, that 'A person is guilty of theft if he dishonestly appropriates property belonging to another, with the intention of permanently depriving the other of it'. The law, being the law, defines each word, each element of the crime. The judges then, pragmatically, define the definitions.

The hardened professional is aware that property has to belong to someone, but it could still amount to theft if property is taken from a person only having possession or control of the item, without being the owner. In fact in some circumstances an owner can be guilty of stealing his own goods. Gas and water can be stolen, as can electricity. Dishonesty is elaborately defined.

A layman can breathe a sigh of relief that whether a person acted dishonestly is to be construed 'according to the ordinary standards of reasonable and honest people'. I wonder what is the modern equivalent of the famed man on the Clapham omnibus – the test of standard behaviour. Perhaps the man or woman having dinner in front of the television set.

Where the professional can have a legal field day is over the words 'intention to deprive the owner permanently'. He may say he was only borrowing the item, intending to return it. Most courts see through this excuse. To be guilty of theft, a person has to have a guilty mind, a dishonest intent.

There remain groups of professional shoplifters, not quite like Dickens' Fagin and his covey of young rascals, but who still usually depend on an outlet for their acquisitions. Hence the police are just as eager to pursue the receivers who handle the wicked fruit of the thief. The receiver, on indictment, can end up sitting in prison long after the thief has been released.

Our criminology departments have still not yet been able to plumb the depths of the mind and soul of the professional criminal. I have spent hours talking to them in my office, or in police cells. Is it something in the genes, in parental influence or lack of it, in the moral climate of the local district or peer group, the failure of schools to instill moral standards? Is it an outbreak of anarchism, retarded intelligence, or an expression of social resentment?

The receiver, the dishonest handler, is in it for the money. The stakes are sometimes very high. One case possibly illustrates why I had few professionals knocking on my door.

My phone rang. It was a lawyer in Tuscany. Could I fly over to Italy to help a client? Within a few days I was ensconced in a smart hotel in a famous seaside resort. I heard the client's story.

He was a fine art dealer in silver, antiques, paintings. He had been arrested in Dover while driving back home.

The car was full of stolen silver. Nothing to do with him. Someone else had put it there. He gave details. The 'someone else' had been arrested. The client had been charged with robbery and dishonest handling.

I listened to a tale of the high life, *la dolce vita*, lived to the full on his visit to London. It was not my world: a world of Rolls-Royces, Ferraris, Aston Martins, all bought and sold as if they were bags of apples; cashmere coats, expensive night clubs, young women always in attendance.

They had left London en route home to Italy when suddenly the police swooped. That journey home ended at Dover. Brought before a London magistrate, a surety appeared out of the blue, guaranteeing a vast sum should the accused fail to return to the court at the next hearing. Bail was granted, conditional on daily reporting at a police station. His passport was surrendered. It was all strange – the story, the surety, the mass of silver. The accused left the court and surfaced a few days later in Italy. Passports were clearly no problem.

The man's wife in Tuscany received mysterious phone calls:

'I am a friend. Do not worry. Everything is taken care of. Do not contact anyone. We want to do it our way. If you want to have your own lawyer, that's OK as long as he collaborates.'

I sat in the hotel lounge in the Italian resort, listening. My private note was the understatement of the year: 'There seems more to the whole matter than appears on the surface'.

What should he do, he asked me as we drank aperitifs. He professed his innocence. I told him to go back and face his accusers

– not the advice he expected or welcomed. Could he, an Italian citizen, be forced back to London, extradited?

I studied the law. It rested on a treaty made between Italy and the United Kingdom for the mutual extradition of fugitive criminals, concluded on 5th February 1873. Despite its title, the treaty said the Italian Government should not deliver up any Italians to the United Kingdom, and no subject of the United Kingdom should be delivered up to the Italian Government. At the time, the United Kingdom had not ratified a subsequent convention, so the 1873 treaty applied. He could not be extradited.

He breathed a sigh of relief. I told him there was nothing to stop the Italian authorities prosecuting him for an offence committed in England. He was not worried. He never took my advice. I was not the type of lawyer he wanted. I returned to England. Italy, though, is always a pleasure to visit.

Not long after, I read of the loss of valuable paintings from an Italian museum – shoplifting on a grand scale. People were arrested for trying to sell them. I recognised something familiar about the facts.

I never heard from the client again. Professional thieves and I clearly did not mix well. He may not have learned much from me, but at least I learned something about extradition law. The spaghetti, however, was excellent – well worth the trip.

Chapter X

Money, Money, Money
or *The Commercial Lawyer*

Introduction

The 1980s were a boom time for the commercial lawyer. Law journals and employment supplements of *The Times* offered aspiring commercial lawyers vast annual salaries, expressed in terms of K rather than £; twice as much as any other breed of lawyer; occasionally six-figure sums. Suddenly, modest firms who hit the commercial jackpot were acquiring imposing City and West End buildings at horrendous rents.

No self-respecting firm failed to have its branches or associated offices strung across the world, wherever a stock exchange tower soared upwards. Partners became millionaires. Legal departments blossomed, involved in tax, company law, European Community law, public share issues, corporate planning, pensions, international employment and immigration law, and intellectual property. The commercial lawyer embraced them all.

This last appellation intrigued me. Intellectual property, I mused, was the God-endowed gift great musicians, painters or artists, scientists, inventors, and authors possessed. Not so. Lawyers saw it as an amalgam of rights and regulations, licences and franchises, copyright, trade marks and trade names, registered designs, patents, computer and software exclusivity – a host of intangibles surrounded by a plethora of Acts, Regulations, Directives, International Conventions, and Treaties.

I was fascinated by the mental precision and acuity of some of my partners, daily engaged in commercial law. For periods I too was a commercial lawyer, but I was inhibited by my theological attitude to money. I say theological, as I ever regarded money as but one episode in the development of the human species.

We enter and leave the planet moneyless. In the great world

beyond, I was sure money did not exist. If we returned to the barter system, or achieved a sophisticated co-operative pattern of mutual support, as envisaged by the early Christians, Essenes, or modern Israel's kibbutzim, then money would indeed be a servant and not a master – a convenient tool.

I often fantasised about the professions, jobs and enterprises that would vanish alongside the abolition of money – accountancy, stock-broking, financial advisers; building societies, insurance companies, banks; Chancellors of the Exchequer, and, of course the commercial lawyer (no fantasy but a nightmare, some would say).

But such fantasies are no help. We have to live in the world we know. For the good life, homes, education, family, health, we need money. I was, therefore, quite happy, at intervals, to be a commercial lawyer. Although acquisitiveness was at their heart, commerce and business intrigued me.

I was always trying my hand at it. In my late teens, a friend and I ran a part-time office service business. In my early twenties I served ice-creams in the kiosk of a seaside restaurant in which my family had an interest, as well as working in a clothing shop in a Kent market town, measuring bodies for suits (men's). A little later I owned a restaurant where the manager decided his financial interest and return should far exceed my own, and where the cooking was, in any event, indeterminate. With the cessation of that business, local health improved.

In 1971, on the very day I went into partnership with long-deceased lawyers Mr O. and Mr G. (represented by their living successors), my partner in a potentially profitable car-hire business suddenly, and unreasonably, decided to join Messrs O. and G. in the world beyond, and I was left with a fleet of cars on my hands, and a business about which I knew nothing.

Thus, although my own Jewish confrères in Britain had produced brilliant businessmen, from Lord Marks to Lord Weinstock, I was never destined to join that august band. I lacked the acumen, the drive, the financial imagination they possessed.

So I settled on advising, like a literary or dramatic critic who comments but does not create; useful, but not original. I formed limited companies, transferred businesses, increased capital, issued debentures, drew up directors and shareholders agreements, transferred shares, often negotiated between contending business partners, drafted and counter-drafted commercial leases, and did my little bit of intellectual property, registering trade marks, trade names, and service marks.

At intervals I entered the realms of higher commercial doctrine. What did the term 'monopoly' mean in the light of European Community legislation? We studied the torrent of legal literature that poured out of Brussels, Strasbourg, Luxembourg. We had to, as our own national courts bowed their heads before the greater sovereignty of the European Court.

As a Privy Council agent I was entitled to practise in the court (or Board) known as the Judicial Committee of the Privy Council, which heard appeals from superior courts of such Commonwealth countries who still regarded London as the *fons et origo* of all legal wisdom. When they were not murder or libel appeals, I was asked to tackle commercial appeals. Lawyers abroad loved these appeals. It meant a trip – all paid – to enjoy the pleasures of the great metropolis.

At other times, weightier issues arose. How was one country going to develop its cotton industry, and protect itself from exploitation and misuse by overseas entrepreneurs? We fought a major action, and for the first time obtained a legal definition of sea island cotton. In the process, a couple of the exhibits were passed to me for personal use. I strongly commend the wearing of apparel made from this natural and sympathetic material. Our intellectual property had become wearable.

The closing down of an insurance company office in England, and the transfer of its policies to both home and overseas companies, set me reading text books and cases. Schemes had to be prepared for judicial sanction. For a time, an actuary and I were the committee running the company. For a year or more we were the company. I rather fancied myself as an insurance mogul, albeit under the watchful eye of the Department of Trade. How remarkable that this industry, with astronomical assets, bestriding the world, began in Mr Lloyd's coffee-shop in the City of London early in the 18th century – another British first.

Then there were the international finance cases. The big commercial law firms glory in these. The firms are enormous. They employ hundreds of solicitors. One American law firm, I was reliably informed, had 750 partners. It was a multinational corporation. Did the partners know one another, and did they have to be introduced? Another fantasy:

'Mr Smith, here is Mr Jones, one of your partners. You ought to get together. He could do something wrong that could ruin you. At least you ought to know him before he gets around to his legal mayhem. Oh yes, there are another 748 of them. If you keep at it, you could meet them all before the decade is out. You should do. They could all ruin you.'

It is reported that 70% of all the lawyers in the world practise in the United States. Japan, rich country that it is, gets by with a handful. Germany, also a wealthy land, has a few more, now grouping together in imitation of the common law Western countries; nothing comparable, though, to England and Wales with their 70,000 solicitors – twice as many as when I began to practise.

More fantasy. Could a new law of economics be formulated, as follows:

a) A country's balance of payments situation is directly related to the number of lawyers practising in that country at any one time.

b) Where the lawyers exceed 20,000 in number, the country will have a serious balance of payments problem.

c) Where the number of practising lawyers exceeds 100,000, that country is really in trouble and the nations accumulated borrowing, combined with its annual balance of payment deficit, should deter any rational man or woman from ever running for president.

The solution to that country's problem is either a rapid increase in public taxation or a rapid decrease in the number of lawyers at work.

d) Any country with less than 20,000 lawyers is blessed, and will prosper for ever.

But the international finance case is waiting. Where better to set it than in Geneva, Switzerland. For six weeks I practically lived in that clean, historic city, delightfully situated on its lake, with a domesticated whale beneath the waters, periodically spouting a great fountain of liquid into the air.

During those six weeks in the late 1980s, I commuted, London to Geneva, Geneva to London. I became an expert on Geneva hotels. Those I didn't stay in I visited. The big financial case is directly linked to the consumption of hotel food – another economic law.

A company owed a consortium millions and millions of pounds.

Another group were prepared to buy the debt at a discount. Simple. Just transfer the debt from consortium to group. To achieve this end, each section of the consortium had previously been advised by merchant banks, or their finance ministries where they were governments. Fortunately they got together and nominated one merchant bank to represent them all. Even more fortunate, they agreed on one London law firm, also mammoth, with their own Smith and Jones, to speak for them all. I represented the buyers.

A major problem was, who had a right to sign for whom? The files were littered with powers of attorney, governmental cabinet decisions, court orders. Formalities became substantive. I couldn't let the clients pay over their fortune until I, and my Geneva colleague, were satisfied to the hilt. We had these wonderful, long, round table meetings. Documents half a metre high weighing several kilograms covered the round table.

Eventually all was settled, naturally, in a banker's elegant office. There were smiles, the inevitable handshakes, and of course, lunch to follow.

I liked being a commercial lawyer. The rewards were substantial. I liked Geneva, just as others trooped off to New York, Hong Kong, Paris, and Frankfurt for the same purpose.

Young people flocked to the commercial cause, bought smart homes and cars on rising incomes. Suddenly the early 1990s produced a recession, the commercial firms began to retract, there were lay-offs and tightening of budgets. Smith and Jones began to feel the chill wind of change.

They might even have had a lunatic thought, got together over a good lunch, and decided to set up a new partnership together. They could advise on commercial law. Who knows? They could make a fortune – one day.

The Story

A deputation of three important civil servants from an overseas country sat in my office. We had never met before, although I knew their country well. We discussed generalities, not quite as banal as the weather, yet nothing really specific. I had a vague idea some action was in the offing as to a major industry back home. Pleasantries continued. They were congenial people. They wanted to know about me. I was uneasy. I was not an applicant for an overseas governmental job. Eventually they expressed a wish to confer on their own.

On my rejoining them they spoke in different terms. They had clearly been interviewing me to see what kind of creature I was. Could I be trusted with confidential information? Did they not know that was the daily lot of solicitors? Integrity, honesty, confidentiality, were the hallmarks of the profession. But these were government secrets. It made no difference to me: government or private individuals. But the merest whisper of certain matters could have political consequences. Agreed, understood.

Leader of the group was head of the Inland Revenue in his country. Despite this, I admired his forthright, clear-headed approach. It was confirmed I would represent his government in the acquisition of the main section of the country's sugar industry. Sugar, at that time, was at the traditional heart of the Caribbean. The word had all kinds of connotations. It represented the main thrust of colonialism, with overtones of slavery, indentured labour, plantation houses, white supremacy. It was, to me, somewhat ironical to be dealing with a sugar issue, as it was Jewish people who first helped bring sugar to the region.

When Jews were expelled from Spain in 1492, and a little later from Portugal, some travelled westward to Recife, in Brazil. As agriculturalists, free to live and worship normally under Dutch control, they experimented with sugar. The long arm of the Inquisition pursued them. As the Portuguese expelled the Dutch, so the Recife Jews were forced to go on their travels once again.

A score journeyed to New Amsterdam (later known as New York) to help in its development. Others scattered throughout the Caribbean basin, bringing with them knowledge of the growing and processing of sugar. This they continued to develop under British and other rulers. In time, sugar became a great source of income for the mother country, much of whose wealth derived from the rich plantations. And so it continued until the Second World War.

After 1945, the campaign of the colonies for independence gathered pace. In the 1960s many in the Caribbean achieved their objective. It was with great rejoicing that independence ceremonies were conducted, Union Jacks lowered, and strangely designed flags of small, new independent nations raised.

Political freedom and independence had been achieved, yet

economic dependence remained. In many of these new sovereign states, industry had been neglected. Goods were bought from the imperial centre, to which primary products went at low protected prices.

With political independence achieved, the new ministers faced vast economic problems. Some relied on tourism to bring in the money. Others, luckier, had natural resources: oil, gas, bauxite. All had sugar. But King Sugar had its own problems.

There was new world competition. Markets were harder to find, even when former colonial powers gave special terms; the European Community had to be convinced; and locals were less and less keen to work in an industry identified with slavery and servitude. Also European beet sugar, processed by the latest technology, was an ever-present threat to the viability of the whole cane sugar industry. Four hundred years after Columbus discovered the New World, Germany, with its scientific beet industry, produced more sugar than all the British Caribbean territories put together.

One of the countries abandoned sugar completely, seeking cotton as a replacement. Few of the others dared copy. The governments tried to assume control of their own economy, to take over ownership of sugar itself. There were economic consequences. There were legal consequences. Hence, the visit of the three wise men bearing questions.

It involved the Stock Exchange in London, the legislature in the acquiring country, a host of negotiations with existing owners, an inventory of assets, debts and debtors, valuations, creation of a new owning company, a prospectus to the public – all the complicated procedure that kept the 750 partner firm in business.

I knew something about the Stock Exchange and allied institutions. One of my best-loved hobbies had been teaching. I had been teaching somebody something most of my life. When my younger son was 16 years old, with examinations ahead, we agreed – school, son and me – that I would teach him a subject then called Commerce. In the process I prepared a set of notes – later in use in his and another school – on the commercial world. Not university standard, but it did take in the Stock Exchange and its procedures. So I knew how precisely accurate a prospectus issued to the public had to be.

There began for us a constant series of eight-man meetings: two of the Government's representatives, two each from the City's largest accountants and brokers, and a partner and myself. We supervised the process. Offers to purchase went out to existing shareholders. Where were they? All over the world. Not all were alive, or, if they were, were not disposed to reply to letters. We had to get a certain percentage to agree to sell before we could force the rest to follow suit, and we needed all the shares.

The price had to be right. Valuations were necessary, balance sheets consulted, future prospects assessed. Throughout, we continued to make obeisance to the Stock Exchange Council, with its holy rules and regulations.

At the same time, the new public company was formed and a prospectus prepared. The Government, determined to decide its own economic future, had already been through similar operations with a foreign-owned telephone system and airline. It had passed enabling legislation through its parliament, but all was not smooth sailing.

The political opposition raised points, as all oppositions rightly do. What was the international outlook for sugar? What guarantee for prices? What value was ascribed to the land, buildings, factories, assets? To answer some of these questions the government needed the wisdom of Solomon, the foresight of Isaiah, and the faith of Job and Jonah. None of them were available. Other expert views were sought and presented.

Political problems went wider. Although the company we were dealing with produced 90% of the country's sugar, there was a host of small peasant producers who sold their cane to the company's factories. What was to be agreed with them? How would they be affected?

I crossed the Atlantic and wandered through some of the sugar factories. A strange sickly smell hung in the atmosphere. Juice extracted from the cane went through a complicated heating and cooling process. The discarded crushed dry cane (bagasse) was used for fuel, whilst from the sugar cane molasses came one of the Caribbean's greatest gifts to mankind – its magnificent rum.

After months of detailed, weekly toil, we had bought in all the shares, formed the new company, agreed every comma of the prospectus, and satisfied the authorities. And lo and behold, at an independence day celebration the High Commissioner rose and, to the delight of his massed nationals, announced that the sugar industry had passed into the people's hands. Great applause and excitement followed, stimulated by one of sugar's favoured by-products. To me, it concluded a complicated, detailed, and, to a limited extent, secretive, legal operation, whose main need was persistence and hard work. A lot was at stake. Detail was all important.

However, to the population of the country, the completion of our involved legal process represented much more. It was like a military victory: the triumph of independence over subservience, of freedom over slavery, of ownership over being owned. The future of sugar might be problematical, but at least it had been repatriated away from the nabobs and their successors in the great mother country. Naturally we celebrated too, with the best liqueur rum.

A year later, another deputation sat in my office. This time it was oil. Our initial interview was shorter and more to the point. The Government was going to take over assets of the company that had first prospected and found oil in its land.

Oil in the 1970s had value far outstripping sugar, or almost any other natural product. Oil was political power. Oil was economic power. The great European oil companies spread their fingers across the globe. They had found this black gold in geological formations from Iraq to Nigeria. They had made themselves rich. The ex-colonial nations wanted that richness for themselves, their people, their future.

We settled down again to technicalities – the how of the operation. The same team was involved. Again valuations, certificates, shares, new companies, the political background. It was fascinating. A new name was found for the national oil company. Parliament legislated. It was a trickier business. Oil companies have all kinds of ancillary agreements, such as transport, servicing. These had to be hived off.

Finally we vested all assets in the newly-formed company and kept the previous company in England as a shell, continued for limited purposes.

Independence day came. Another function. 'We now own our own oil.' Cheers, enthusiasm. Another blow for economic independence. It called for a celebration, drunk naturally in another kind of liquid gold. I liked these complicated commercial cases. In fact I quite liked being a commercial lawyer, but not for too long. I was not sure my stomach could contend with the diet, or the drink, especially the drink.

Chapter XI

The Good Lord and the Tribunal

Introduction

It was 11th April 1981. There had been riots in Brixton. The Home Secretary had rushed to this south London suburb to inspect the damage, the looting, the smashed windows. An inquiry would be held, he announced.

I had been away from London that unusually warm spring weekend. My wife and I had won a free holiday in one of England's gourmet establishments on the south coast, a prize for winning a quiz on the history and geography of Kent, England's 'garden'.

It was peaceful in our hotel on the edge of the New Forest in Hampshire, enjoying the memorable meals, wandering through the shaded paths beneath towering pines, surveying the calm, distant sea. We glanced at the television. The assembled guests could not believe their eyes. Street rioting was taking place on a scale never before seen in Britain, at least this century.

I was shocked at the destruction, the rage, the fires, the street battles, but not surprised that there had been this eruption. The world of our fashionable hotel and its polite guests was 60 miles away, and at the same time several light-years, from the teeming tenements of black Brixton, with their poverty, their tension, their sense of siege in the face of heavy-handed policing, as well as incitement from the extreme left and right of the political spectrum.

It was a world I understood. The guests pointed out that the rioters were black. Black is an American term. Those who came to Britain from the West Indies were Jamaicans, Barbadians, Guyanese, and so on. They had a national identity. Black is a colour, not an identity. It is a political term used to describe a minority in the United States in the 1960s, who previously called themselves Negroes, coloured people, and, much later, Afro-Americans, but then described themselves as black, in contrast to white Americans. The description had been imported to Britain, and became common parlance.

I was shocked, but not surprised. I had known danger was building up, as a result of my constant contact with the West Indian world. I had been deeply concerned for some time. In 1977 I formed a committee, composed of an MP, magistrates, community relations experts, to highlight the problem of that minority and amass chapter and verse as to their grievances.

The material we collated was accurate and impressive. We met in 1979 with the Minister of State at the Home Office and his officials. We set out a precise historical statement as to the cause of problems, and a number of detailed proposals to reverse a rapidly deteriorating situation. We told the Minister that our efforts represented the last chance the Government had to prevent an explosion. We agreed to keep our dialogue out of the public eye, despite probing from the media, so that the Minister's actions, based on our proposals, would not be seen as bowing to public pressure.

The Minister said he would consider the matter seriously. He did, but then wrote to me at length, politely, full of fine phrases, without the slightest sense of urgency or understanding of what was at stake. It was 'Civil Servicese' at its most fluent and plausible, yet totally uncomprehending of the real world.

I replied that we had clearly failed to impress on him the seriousness of the situation. The Government, the departmental mentality, the institutionalised remoteness, all contributed to a missed opportunity of major proportions. Within 20 months the ghettoes exploded, not only in Brixton.

A strange characteristic can be observed in this remarkable, pragmatic country. People usually have to get injured or killed before authorities sit up and take notice. There are numerous examples of this national myopia: dangerous drugs, environmental spillage, aircraft crashes, Clapham trains, Zeebrugge ferries, Thames riverboats. After each disaster there is an inquiry, a hurried review, then frequently a rapid change of laws and procedures. One day matters could be reversed. How splendid it would be if inquiries could be initiated on a comprehensive scale long before any disaster struck. That needs vision. Busy politicians rarely have time for such a commodity.

The Brixton riots took place and hurriedly produced a tribunal, known subsequently as the Scarman Inquiry. Lord Scarman presided. I was one of the advocates. The eyes of the country watched and waited. We had reached a watershed in group relations in Britain. What would emerge? Many hopes centred on this tall, gaunt, courteous judge, known for his liberal outlook on and off the bench, and his concern for human beings and human rights. For me, contact with Lord Scarman was an illuminating stage in my continuing education.

The Story

It was a clear morning, June 1981, the first day of the inquiry. I decided to reach Lambeth Town Hall early. The hearing would not begin before 10.30 a.m. I arrived two hours early. A few cleaners were finishing. Local staff and workmen sauntered unhurriedly along the Edwardian corridors of this undistinguished red brick town hall. No solicitors, no barristers, no advocates, were to be seen. They were sensible people. They would arrive at sensible times.

I entered the large, cavernous, well-lit chamber, useful for public meetings, stage plays and concerts, but converted into a strange kind of oversized court.

The judge would sit alone, slightly elevated. To his left, witnesses would stand, or sit, to give evidence. In a huge wall-to-wall semi-circle, straddling the entire width of the ample hall, facing the judge, stood large tables, eight or nine of them, each allotted to one or more legal representatives of the particular groups involved. To the far right of the judge was the table of Treasury Counsel, presenters of the evidence. Behind the tables, row upon row of chairs were lined up for public use, extending to the rear entrance doors, whilst in far corners all manner of radio, television, and recording equipment was installed. Provision was made for the press.

All was quiet and still that early morning in what was later to become an arena for strong passions and heated words. I wondered which table was for us. I had an assistant with me. We deposited our papers on a likely-looking table; likely that is not to collapse under the vast quantity of documents that had poured into our office during the preceding few months.

I thought we were alone. I looked around and noticed a spare figure wandering from table to table, checking that chairs, glasses, water containers (for parched throats), signs, and equipment were all in order; that the physical comfort of public, press, and professionals had been catered for; that equal and suitable provision had been provided for all participants.

That was my first encounter with Lord Scarman. We spoke, not about the difficult task ahead, especially for him, but about chairs and tables, lighting and heating. We could have been a couple of surveyors, checking an inventory, the condition of a building, but there we were, one judge, one advocate,

In due course others drifted in, but I pondered the quality of this man of judicial distinction, Appeal Court judge, noted commentator on legal issues, wandering about in the early morn to make sure the physical comforts of all those who, an hour or two later, would defer to him had been satisfactorily considered. It was an object lesson in humility and sense of service in a profession so often afflicted by arrogance and self-importance.

On the evening of 10th April 1981, a young West Indian was stabbed in a fight in Brixton. Police officers found him, put him in the back of their car, and began to bind up what, to them, looked like a serious wound, at the same time radioing for medical help.

It sounded like one of the problems police have to deal with which happen all too often in these days of increased violence. The officers, from their experience, thought it would be dangerous to move the young man before expert medical help arrived.

Several hundred West Indian youths (or so it seemed to witnesses) gathered around the car. They saw police officers doing something to the shoulder of one of their 'brothers'. They suspected either wrongful police action, or unnecessary delay in getting the young man to the hospital. Acting as a group, they took the law into their own hands, and forcibly removed the injured young man from the police, saying, 'We will look after our own'.

This was the ostensible, immediate incident that triggered off three days of riots, arson, attacks on police with petrol bombs, police attacks on civilians, looting and hostility, probably unparalleled in a British city within living memory. It was like a war.

On Saturday 11th April, the following day, a police officer stopped a West Indian he suspected of stuffing some unlawful material into one of his socks. The police officer suspected a breach of the law; it turned out to be otherwise, but meanwhile another confrontation developed, with the officer surrounded by an antagonistic group of West Indians. This triggered off further violence on that day.

Brixton became a battlefield, with charges and counter-charges, casualties, removal of consumer goods en masse from shops – televisions, radios, record-players – screaming ambulances and fire-engines criss-crossing the battle area, frightened families – white and black – caught up in some hideous nightmare.

It was not until Monday 13th April that the violence ceased, and an unwritten truce emerged between the contending parties.

When the intense and unforgiving heat of passion had subsided, both sides began to count the cost. A major shopping centre had been stripped and ransacked. A campaign by older West Indians and local community relation bodies to develop constructive dialogue with the police lay in ruins. The police themselves, untrained for this kind of emergency, suffered casualties. Houses had been set on fire.

The riots had attracted the lawless from other parts of London. Self-appointed minority leaders used the events to castigate the police and all forms of authority, even the country itself. They called the violence an 'uprising', referred to 'the front-line'. The terminology of war dominated. Similar battles erupted elsewhere, notably Toxteth in Liverpool.

The British public were shocked. Parliament and the Cabinet were shocked. The world had seen on television screens outbursts of lawlessness and hate in law-abiding, civilised Britain. Members of the West Indian community were themselves shocked, though many had perceived some of the hidden fires that had risen so furiously to the surface. Why had this happened, been allowed to happen? People wanted answers. A formal inquiry was demanded, and thus the problem passed into the calm and capable hands of Lord Scarman.

The inquiry was set up under the Police Act, 1964, to enquire into methods of policing, especially in multi-racial areas. It started in mid-June, and lasted over three weeks, with a further week in September 1981. The first part dealt with the incidents themselves; the second with underlying causes. There were oral hearings, at which witnesses gave evidence, and were questioned, based on written statements previously taken. In addition, all parties prepared written evidence, and, quite apart from the eight or nine organisations represented, written statements poured in on Lord Scarman from individuals and organised bodies, statutory and otherwise, from all over the country.

Throughout, the good Lord presided with impeccable fairness, calmness, good humour, and acute perception, as well as tolerance of the foibles and prejudices of individuals, allowing many issues to be raised beyond those of policing methods and attitudes.

He was frequently provoked, often by lines of questioning and political harangues aimed more at the media, the West Indian public in the room, and at the communal and political office and ambition of those involved, rather than directed at the facts in issue. Lord Scarman was aware that a great head of steam had to be given an outlet: hence he allowed expressions and questions that might have been frowned upon elsewhere.

Gradually the quality I had detected early on the first morning pervaded the proceedings. His natural courtesy, sense of equality, and scrupulously polite manner of address brought dignity and reason into an inflamed world of contention and recrimination.

As witness followed witness, day after day, week after week – police, journalists, social workers, councillors, Members of Parliament, doctors, firemen, ambulance men, shopkeepers, community workers – a picture emerged of sharply contrasting attitudes and beliefs, of bitter fractiousness, of steady unremitting friction that eventually ignited, of an eagerly-accepted mythology, of the darting power of rumour, of the enormous complexity, often mindlessness, of group reactions.

We lawyers questioned endlessly. I represented the Council of Community Relations of Lambeth, itself a body to which 80 local organisations were affiliated. To my left sat John Hazan QC (subsequently an Old Bailey judge) representing the police. To my right sat Louis Blom-Cooper, also a QC (subsequently knighted), and one who was later to preside over several inquiries of public importance. The fact that I, as a solicitor, and they, as barristers, were engaged on the same process, on the same level, and regarded each other in the same light, was as it should be – an indication of that movement towards equality in the profession that has long been overdue.

We were enquiring into policing, especially in areas with a multi-racial population. As days passed, the police appeared to be more and more on the defensive. Why they should have been was, on the face of it, unclear, since they did not riot, but had tried to maintain law and order in their own way.

The police were the smallest minority group in Brixton, but a minority with considerable power. They were almost all white in an area where about a quarter of the population was black West Indian.

Their training had not prepared them for the proper understanding of minority groups, not surprising, as there were at least a dozen such groups living locally.

The force was organised on semi-military lines, with a hierarchical pattern of command. Its job was to prevent crime, maintain the Queen's peace, apprehend criminals. It had never seen itself as a social service body, a welfare group, or having any functions other than those mentioned.

From the police viewpoint – reflected in much of the evidence of the officers – there had been an alarming rise in local street crime, committed by young men of West Indian origin. To combat this, campaigns were launched, like the strangely named 'Swamp 81', with a high concentration of stop-and-search operations – a major cause of resentment – and a special patrol group brought in from outside to conduct a kind of anti-crime blitzkrieg.

Also the police suspected extremist political incitement by those intent on anti-police, anti-authority agitation to further political ends.

With some exceptions, they also suspected the local Community Relations Council (CRC) officers, self-defeatingly arresting some of them on the CRC premises – arrests without any real foundation – thus effectively destroying lines of communication desperately needed. That was the police viewpoint, however.

The CRC officers, on the other hand, felt the police were insensitive, short-sighted, not endeavouring to police by consent, not developing adequately the responsibilities of the home-beat officer, not treating them with due respect.

How did the West Indian community, on the other hand, see the position? I use the expression 'West Indian', although two of the barristers representing one group saw it as a Jamaican community in the district, rather than a West Indian one. There are undoubtedly differing strands within that community, especially relating to country of origin.

Their general attitude could be summarised thus: life was not easy, housing conditions were bad, jobs scarce, there was little to hope for, time hung heavy, with limited leisure facilities, much congregating took place on streets, above all, they felt the constant pressure of institutionalised hostility, especially from the police, making daily life uncertain, unsettled, within an overall climate of fear and confrontation.

This showed itself in what was widely regarded as police abuse of the 'sus' laws as to loitering with intent (activated under the archaic Vagrancy Act, 1824, subsequently repealed), in unauthorised breaking into premises, in lack of civility, respect, and simple courtesy in approach, in reports of unprovoked assaults in police stations. Thus a stereotyped picture of the police was built up, based partly on fact and partly on myth. Suspicion became endemic, especially among the younger men. The older generation, who had long disbelieved reports of police wrongdoing, began to see the position in the same light as their children.

It was useless to file complaints of official misbehaviour, as police were judges in their own cause. Complaints usually aggravated the initial problem.

Thus when two police officers on that Friday night in April tried to help the youngster in the car, these background forces were at work. Consciously or unconsciously, they affected how each group saw and interpreted the actions of the other.

What was in the hearts and minds of each group led to the eruption of hatred, antagonism and physical violence; the product of bad community relations over a long period, and a lack of understanding, of communication, between two groups.

There may have been other factors, either more profound or more speculative. A number were raised at the inquiry, for example, the effect on human behaviour of the high lead content of the atmosphere in Lambeth or the sudden and unusual burst of hot weather on that April weekend, and the irrationality of group behaviour generally.

Eventually, closing speeches were made, proposals for change submitted. Lord Scarman went away and pondered. In due course his report appeared, a milestone in British policy and in the development of community relations.

Police colleges responded with new training programmes. Police consultative committees were set up locally to cement dialogue, enlarge mutual perceptions, as well as encourage new forms of joint activities between police and community. A new beginning emerged that gave hope for the future, even though that future was, at intervals, punctuated by lesser eruptions of group violence. One day we will really understand the archetypal, almost atavistic, psyche of group behaviour, and rise above the infectious fear, the uncontrolled passion, that grip and dominate otherwise sensible and rational individuals.

I had, at the inquiry, met, in the early morning of the opening day, one who had risen far above the group longing for a scapegoat, the primitivism of the baying crowd, the wavers of banners and chanters of slogans. I had met a decent, cultured man who cared, and who, by words and demeanour, also cured. I had met a man, who, in his judicial role at the head of the inquiry, and in his profoundly humane approach to all people, irrespective of colour or creed, had helped to bind up deep wounds that, having festered long, had burst forth in all their rawness and ferocity in the body politic. I had met a really good man.

Chapter XII

Bangladesh – A Commission of Enquiry

Introduction

Only in the second half of this century have women begun to make their mark politically, after much agitation during the first half of the century. As a result, exceptional women have risen to the top of the political tree.

Women prime ministers have presided in Norway, Great Britain, Israel, France, and other Western democracies. Remarkable too is the rise to prominence of women in the East, in newly independent countries, Indira Gandhi in India, Benazir Bhutto in Pakistan, Mrs Bandaranaike in Sri Lanka – all prime ministers.

I was not surprised therefore to see a potential women president or prime minister sitting opposite me in my office in the early 1980s. Short, impressive, clear-minded, Sheikh Hasina Wazed of Bangladesh came from a political family. Her father, Sheikh Mujibur Rahman, had been the father of his nation.

The state of Bangladesh was born in 1972 in great travail, out of what previously had been East Pakistan. In 1947, when, to Mahatma Gandhi's sorrow, the subcontinent split into the independent states of India and Pakistan, the two separate parts of the latter were divided by one thousand miles of the Indian homeland. It was an impossible political entity. The eastern part, Bengal, sought independence, and achieved it eventually with Indian help, to the detriment of Indo-Pakistan relations.

The future of this low-lying, frequently-flooded state was fraught with problems from its birth. Its one hundred and twenty million souls, an enormous population for so poor a country, have had to fight the onslaught of nature at the same time as the instability of its leadership. Yet good forces were at work. My experience was with one of them.

Sheikh Mujib had been assassinated in a coup by army officers three years after the foundation of the state. No one had been prosecuted, no enquiries had been made. An international commission of inquiry was set up in London to discover why the criminals had not been brought to justice. This is the story of that commission.

The Story

Sheikh Hasina Wazed and her supporters told me of their problems. Her Awami League party sought a liberal, left-of-centre, secular state. They did not want the religious elite or the military to dominate. The new constitution guaranteed basic human rights and freedoms. Her father, the first president, had tried to guide the country along those lines. There was opposition, accusations, agitation. Many who had cheered rapturously for independence found its achievement had barely altered their condition.

In countries with long democratic traditions, rules and governments change peacefully through the sovereignty of the ballot box; but in the tension of Bangladesh, amidst the ambitions of competing soldiers and politicians, that was not the way things happened.

Mujib had been brutally murdered. On 15th August 1975 a group of army officers with hundreds of men burst into the President's home. They must have been berserk. Not only did they murder Mujib, but also his wife and sons, his brother, brother-in-law, children aged 3 and 4 years, visiting guests to the house, servants; twenty-two people in all.

It had the ring of the brutal parts of the Old Testament or pagan legends where not merely one, but several generations were killed to prevent any future dynastic claimant arising.

A few months later, on 3rd November 1975, these same army officers burst into the central jail in Dacca, capital city of Bangladesh, and attacked four men who had been held there following the coup on 15th August 1975 by General Zia ur-Rahman. The four men were brutally murdered, among them a former vice-president and former prime ministers.

In September, shortly after Mujib's murder, while martial law reigned, an ordinance was promulgated which had the effect of indemnifying the murderers from any legal proceedings provided the new President issued a certificate justifying previous action taken.

The whole saga was too cynical, too horrifying, for words. As if the depths had not been plumbed, the officers involved in both murders, despite public admissions as to their guilt, were given diplomatic posts abroad, mainly in Muslim countries. Two of them went to live in Libya – not the world's greatest exponent of human rights.

Sheikh Wazed campaigned for action to be taken against the self-confessed murderers of her father. Nothing was done.

Two years later, in 1977, Sean McBride of Ireland led an Amnesty International mission to Bangladesh, and was told by President Zia, 'The law will take its course'. The law took no course at all. In fact Zia was himself murdered in 1981.

Sheikh Wazed gave me all the documents, all the reports. They made grim reading. The state had been born in 1972 in a mood of hope. Mujib had been acclaimed as the father of his nation, given the affectionate title of Bangabandhu. He had inspired the people towards independence.

His policy was based on four pillars: nationalism and the national culture of Bengal, based on the philosophy of humanism of the great philosopher and poet Tagore; democracy; secularism, so that no religion would dominate the state; and socialism, which he saw as a means of retaining the wealth of the country for its people.

Every effort had been made to thwart him. He had been tried for conspiracy, a charge that failed. He had been imprisoned. The fight for independence had lasted for nine blood-filled months. When independence came, the new nation rejoiced in its freedom and in its first president.

Yet within three years this man, born in humble circumstances, had been gunned down. I wanted to know more about him. His daughter handed me a booklet. It recorded speeches at a meeting held in the House of Commons on 15th August 1980, the fifth anniversary of her father's death.

The booklet contained speeches and messages recorded at that gathering. Her father had been held in the highest regard by leaders of all political parties, from Sir Edward Heath to Michael Foot. Sheikh Wazed herself had written:

'My father's vision was of a Bangladesh free of religious bigotry, socially emancipated, politically mature. That dream, when transformed into reality, will be his most enduring monument.'

Sir Thomas Williams QC, MP, spoke of Mujib's courage, of his faith in his people, of his dedication to democracy. Dr Kemal Hossein, former foreign minister, spoke of the deceased President's vision of a society free from exploitation.

I asked Sheikh Wazed what she wished me to do. She replied that she wanted me to help in setting up a commission of inquiry, and to be a member of the commission. The chairman would be Sir Thomas Williams, who later sat as a judge at the Old Bailey. The other members of the commission were my good friend Jeffrey Thomas, a QC and MP; Sean McBride, the famous Irishman, who had the unusual distinction of holding both the Lenin Prize and the Nobel Prize for Peace; and Dr Kemal Hossein in his capacity as a member of the International Commission of Jurists.

Our commission was set up, duly announced at a press conference, and we met to plan our programme. We set out a series of questions to be answered, primarily why due process of law did not follow the murders, whether the indemnity law was constitutional, whether any certificates of indemnity had ever been issued, and what action would be taken by the Bangladesh authorities.

The proposal for our commission apparently had widespread support. Funds had been raised among Bangladeshis abroad, particularly in England, to support the inquiry. Feeling ran high in east London, where most of the Bangladeshi community here lived. There had been public meetings, resolutions, appeals. British MPs had added their voices to the campaign. Some had been close friends of Mujib and were aghast at his death, and its significance for the future of democracy in his land.

I attended meetings in Parliament with sympathetic MPs, and also gatherings in east London. It was decided that Jeffrey Thomas would visit Dacca. A series of meetings had been arranged for him. He would be our representative. He would go with our authority, and would report back to us. The Bangladeshi Government was informed, as was the British Foreign Office.

Travel arrangements were completed, a visa was promised, but at the very last moment, it became clear that, on instructions presumably from Dacca, no visa was to be issued. The Foreign Office intervened. The matter was raised in the House of Lords. Nothing could be done. It was a studied snub and insult by a scared government who feared an investigation.

When the news emerged that no visa had been issued, there were protest meetings in Bangladesh, and 10,000 people took part in a march in Dacca. We decided to prepare a report in any event, and to hold a press conference to announce its contents.

We assembled for the conference in a large hall, formerly used as a Jewish communal centre. It was filled to capacity, not merely with Bangladeshis, but with the press, the radio, BBC World Service, everyone we could get along from the media. Due to parliamentary commitments, the MP members of the commission could not attend.

What an extraordinary scene it was: cameras flashing, microphones held close, reporters taking notes, a crowd of eager Bangladeshis. And who were the spokesmen for their cause? An Irishman and a Jew – Sean McBride and myself!

Strange world, the law. You never know what tomorrow may bring. You're not too sure about today. It was a gathering that remains vividly in my mind for its passion, and for the strange incongruity of these two commissioners announcing findings to the media and to the world.

The assassins were never brought to justice. The president who tried to protect them was himself removed. Sheikh Wazed went on later to fight an election in her country for the office of Prime Minister, only to be beaten... by another woman. How delighted I was that at a subsequent election in 1996 Sheikh Wazed won and became Prime Minister. The wheel had turned full circle. She now had the chance to build on the foundations her father had established.

In 1993 Dr Kemal Hossein and I reflected together on those tense days a decade or more earlier. We were the only survivors of the commission. The others had passed on.

I was intrigued to learn from him subsequently that the case was still open and under review, especially the legality of the indemnity law. Perhaps the climate of opinion in Bangladesh had changed, and the ideals of human rights and the rule of law acknowledged with a greater sense of urgency and understanding. If so, it would be a fitting tribute to the memory of a courageous leader of his people.

Chapter XIII

The Bubble Reputation

Introduction

William Shakespeare, who understood most things, language especially, perceived the deep grief caused by an unscrupulous use of words in assaulting a person's reputation. For libel, and its junior partner slander, are a form of assault, oftentimes more profoundly wounding than any physical injury. Regard in *Othello*, Cassio's *cri de coeur*: 'Reputation, reputation, reputation! O! I have lost my reputation. I have lost the immortal part of myself and what remains is bestial.'

The cynical Iago, surely a defendant's favourite for a libel jury trial, responds: 'Reputation is an idle and most false imposition; oft got without merit, and lost without deserving; you have lost no reputation at all unless you repute yourself such a loser.'

Libel actions are demanding. I have been involved in many. We lawyers deal often with intangibles, emotions, ideals, translated into practical legal consequences, yet when a person's reputation is in issue, we are handling the very essence of a being. Cassio felt he had lost 'the immortal part of myself'; somewhat of an over-statement, reflecting, however, his overwhelming sense of loss, of being reduced as a person. It is right therefore that the law should punish the defamer and compensate the defamed.

Criminal libel used to hold sway, but is little in evidence today. Very much in evidence, though, is the increasing volume of civil claims seeking damages for libel. We now have a body of lawyers who deal with hardly anything else – libel lawyers.

As, in the criminal law, a person is deemed innocent until proven guilty, so, in the eyes of English law, everyone starts off with a good name and a right to retain it. Also, as the law loves certainty and definition, it defines a defamatory statement. This is 'one which tends to lower a person in the estimation of right-thinking members of society generally, or to cause him/her to be shunned or avoided, or expose him/her to hatred contempt or ridicule'.

Clearly this opens the way for a host of interpretations. We are back on the Clapham omnibus, with the ordinary, reasonable man, and how he understands the meaning of words. One hopes the ladies and gentlemen of the jury are omnibus people, with their feet on the ground (when they alight), and aware too of the rapid change in society of what is regarded as defamatory. *Autre temps, autre* libels.

Libel is defamation in a permanent form, usually in writing or print, on a film soundtrack, on radio, in a play, even in a statue or an inscription on a tombstone. In libel the law assumes damage. Slander is defamation in a non-permanent form, invariably the spoken word, and specific damage has to be proved.

A bank marking a cheque 'return to drawer' when there is money in the account to meet payment may find itself sued for damages, as can anyone asserting wrongly that a person suffers from certain diseases. The possibilities seem endless. Libel laws, for some, are a passport to a treasure house of easily-gained, non-taxable money. The libel litigant can leave a court laughing, or weeping, all the way to the bank.

Cases are enormously expensive, ridiculously expensive. How often is an award of substantial damages dwarfed by the legal costs involved. There must be a more sensible method of securing a citizen's reputation, especially when that person is poor, or of limited means, or opposed by a rich newspaper or corporation.

That eminent solicitor, Lord Goodman, in his book *Tell Them I Am On My Way* (Chapmans), expresses himself in no uncertain terms: 'I strongly urge that a libel action, with its increasing cost as the years go by, with its appalling delays, and with the uncertainty of a jury verdict, is a demented adventure by most people and should only be resorted to when the affront is so gross that no self-respecting person can ignore it.' And that from one of our most experienced, gifted and perceptive practitioners.

I once acted for an honest upright man, mercilessly pilloried on the front page of a national newspaper, who was too frightened to embark on litigation because of the costs involved. This is not justice, done, seen to be done, heard to be done. It is justice undone. Press councils and commissions have so far been ineffective. One day not only the privacy laws, but the libel laws and their enforcement will receive a radical overhaul.

Meanwhile, sums awarded mount extravagantly, often into many hundred of thousands of pounds. I have read in newspapers of large damages awarded to people for attacks on their reputation, when I was aware those people had no reputation to lose. Libel actions for some have become a business, a form of investment. Occasionally actions collapse when an intensive and expensive investigation, backed by a rigorous cross-examination, exposes a claimant's sham reputation. 1997 saw one such case of a dramatic nature.

Textbooks on the subject, ever expanding in content, talk of 16 possible defences. These range from absence of publication of the libel to a third party, the truth of the allegation, fair comment on a matter of public interest (the newspaper's friend), absolute privilege (words spoken by MPs in the course of the parliamentary process, or by those taking part in a court case), to qualified privilege (a trickier defence where a mutual duty to disclose information and an interest in hearing it coincide).

By the time all parties get to court, the issues have been set out in documents. The plaintiff's counsel rises and outlines his client's case. Sometimes he reminds the jury of the Bard's well-known words, 'he that filches from me my good name robs me of that which not enriches him and makes me poor indeed'.

The evidence and speeches of both sides end. The judge decides if there is evidence of defamation for the jury to consider. The jury decide if the person is defamed, and how much to award as damages. The case concludes, one party wreathed in smiles, congratulating lawyers, the other party aghast at the consequences of the legal process.

Outside, reporters congregate. The victor declares his faith in British justice, that his decision was a complete vindication of his decision to bring proceedings in order to clear his good name. The loser slinks off, shaking his or her head at the gullibility or contrariness of the jury, and is soon closeted with lawyers as to an appeal, or with bank managers as to overdraft facilities. It happens so often.

Sometimes I wonder how the characters in the holy books of the various religions would have been affected had our libel laws then been in force. It is a tempting exercise. They used some strong language. But such reveries are for other times.

I recall to mind however, three cases, whose motives were, respectively, political, sensation seeking, and mercenary, and which illustrate the workings of this very active section of the law, guardian of the citizen's reputation. We no longer fight duels with swords to uphold our reputations. Today we leave it to the lawyers, but a goodly number still leave the field with wounds and scars that remain for many a year.

The Story

The Minister

It happened on a beautiful Caribbean island. Palm trees waved over golden sands, beckoning to the clear blue sea. The populace were peaceful, courteous, fairly industrious. Transition to independence in the 1960s had been without incident, with joy and celebration. A stable democratic political process ruled. The judiciary was respected and independent. And the sun, which shone most of the time, brought not only light, but heat, modified by the cooling trade winds. It smacked of paradise.

Then came the general election. As the political temperature rose the governing party produced a journal which ascribed unacceptable motives to the two main opposition leaders. The accusation was that, over and above their fees (so many politicians were lawyers), they had a personal financial interest in a case in which they were engaged. Their integrity and honesty were impugned. They were referred to as 'fat cats'. The article should never have been published in its raw form. It went out unchecked through a chapter of accidents.

But all concerned with publication had to accept responsibility. Even a subsequent apology was delayed and mismanaged. Newspapers can limit responsibility by a quick and complete printed correction and expression of regret. It did not happen.

As matters turned out the Prime Minister (who chaired the publishing company) and his party were re-elected. The Leader of the Opposition, one of the two defamed, actually won a seat he had never stood for previously, whilst his colleague lost his seat, but later become a senator and Prime Minister. One recipient of a writ was the Speaker of the Legislature, who, before the election, was editor of the offending journal.

We had a fascinating time representing him and his party colleagues, including research as to how far a Speaker could be sued for libel over an article for which he had responsibility at the time, but whose offending words he had never read in the heat of electoral activity before they were issued to the world.

The parties also involved – Prime Minister, Opposition leaders – were splendid men. I knew them all, respected them all. But within days of the appearance of the article writs flew. The island's High Court deliberated, pondered, and finally found for the plaintiffs.

The words complained of, it confirmed, had undoubtedly lowered them in the eyes of right-thinking people. The court found imputations that the complainants were unpatriotic (significant in a newly independent state), sought improper financial gain, displayed professional impropriety, were unfit to be elected as legislators, and even discovered, in the rash of words, a dash of treason (a finding speedily removed on appeal).

Meanwhile, the Government governed, the palm trees waved, and the blue seas of the Caribbean continued their gentle ebb and flow across warm sunlit sands.

Eventually, as years passed, the case wound its way to the Queen's Most Excellent Majesty in Council in London, the Judicial Committee of the Privy Council, hearers of appeal from courts where the sun never sets, at least in those days.

Two issues had to be decided. Damages awarded were a record for the country. Surely they were too high? Aggravated damage the law called it. Her Majesty's Board of Advisers in London wouldn't intervene. No principle had been breached. An earlier apology would have helped. The damages remained inviolate.

The second point concerned the meaning or implication of the words used in the article. Were they to be construed as understood locally, or generally in the world? Again, no help from the lofty judges, who, incidentally, sat in dark suits, without the aid of wigs or gowns, and were none the worse for it: they were not lowered in my estimation by this sartorial preference, possibly even raised. Their Lordships in mufti queried, 'If local judges agree on the meaning of wording can we interfere?' Though put as a question, as judges often do, it was in fact a decision.

That was that. Appeal dismissed. Back to the sunshine. The word went out from London. An imposing sheet of grey paper with seal embossed was issued 'at the Court at Buckingham Palace' stating that the Queen had accepted the advice of her Judicial Committee to dismiss the appeal and was mightily pleased 'by and with the advice of Her Privy Council' to approve it, ordering 'that the same be punctually observed obeyed and carried into execution'. The wording even enjoined 'the Governor General, or officer administering the Government (of the Commonwealth country), to take notice and govern themselves accordingly'.

Delightful wording, pleasantly archaic, almost Gilbertian, or am I being unpatriotic, even displaying a touch of treason? I hope not. I hold the Queen in great respect. That was the end of the case; a legal divertissment, a fall-out from general election fever.

The beautiful island carried on with its business. Tourists poured in, enjoying sun, sand, sea, and rum punches. Parliament went about its business. The politicians involved in the case went from strength to strength, became national and international figures of note. They continued to talk to each other, debate with each other.

The issue passed into local lore as the 'fat cats' case, for those offending words in the article had particularly stuck in the gullet. It is now history for the textbooks and students. Visitors from colder northern climes, lazing on golden beaches at the time, had not the faintest idea of the turbulence then agitating the local leaders. Just as well, since politics and suntans, elections and poolside barbecues, do not mix.

As the years elapsed, the Prime Minister, then so embroiled and embattled, was revered by all as the father and founder of his nation, just as public respect for his opponents at the time climbed likewise. Reputation, reputation. O! my reputation.

The Mayor

When Joseph Addison, early in the 1700s, wrote his elegant essays for *The Spectator*, commenting gently, satirising mildly the social mores of his day, he could not have imagined the ferocity of his journalistic colleagues of the late 20th century. Instead of extracts in Latin from the classical works of Ovid and Horace, the public are today presented with unexpurgated quotations from private documents, however indelicate the language; tape recordings of personal conversations, however intimate; headlines full of suggestive and wicked hyperbole, spread-eagled across the face of the world on the often doubtful justification of being 'in the public interest' or 'matters of public concern'.

Whilst this new investigative journalism, properly prepared, researched, and published, can be of service and value to the reading and voting public, it is swamped by the free market in prurience, innuendo, and misinformation that dominates some of the daily papers of the Western world. Freedom of expression is a precious jewel, a right that implies a corresponding duty, a sense of responsibility, of respecting feelings and sensitivities.

I was therefore appalled by a newspaper thrust before me by a deeply saddened couple. A thick black, glaring headline dominated the front page, 'Extortion by Mayor Allegation'. The article beneath contained every emotive word imaginable, extending to implications of blackmail. Some journalist, some editor, eyes possibly on circulation and sensation, had let loose a farrago of untruths on several hundred thousand readers.

The couple with me were the Mayor and Mayoress of a prominent London borough. I had known them for years; deeply religious Christians, public-spirited in work for charities and local government, devoted to their family, professionals in the teaching and care of children, innocent victims of a barrage of malicious and dangerous accusations.

They were so hurt – pierced – by the words, that it was almost too much for them to respond coherently. The attack was beneath contempt, but they soon realised that to do nothing would give encouragement to the nonsensical 'no smoke without fire' brigade. Hence we sat together to consider how best to react.

I am a believer in getting around a table and reasoning together. We tried it with the editor and his lawyer, gave them the chance to make amends without recourse to the courts. We explained the seriousness of the matter. They prevaricated, delayed, hoped we would never proceed, possibly misinterpreted our reasonableness. They paid dearly for their stratagems.

Writs descended on the owner of the journal, the editor, the reporters, the printer, the distributor – all party to the defamation of its publication. They rushed forward to settle. We were in no hurry. Our claim was formidable.

'By reason of the publication the plaintiffs have suffered grievous embarrassment and anxiety and each have been gravely injured in their reputations and been brought into public scandal, odium and contempt.'

So ran the claim. Every word was true. There was no defence. They suggested a form of apology. We rejected it. We prepared our own words, 'the charges were unfounded..., the article should never have been published..., allegations withdrawn without reservation..., apologise for distress caused..., substantial damages..., costs...'.

They grovelled in court. Our wording appeared prominently in their next issue. Yet how could one quantify financially the hurt caused by such irresponsibility? Would the apology be seen by everyone who had read the original article? But how vital it was that we had the avenue of the courts to walk. The process of law, with all its defects, is still a great civiliser, provided it is not abused. Without it there is no redress except recourse to violence.

The issue ended speedily. Yet why do editors and reporters behave in such a despicable way? Did the editor, dominated by circulation figures, pray 'Give us this day our daily sensation?' It is so sad, so utterly irresponsible, so heartless.

The Mayor, relieved, went back to his council chamber, his head high, restored to respect. The Mayoress returned to caring for children. An ugly episode ended. It need never have taken place. I wondered if the paper, its editor and reporters, had learned any lessons. I hoped they had. Libel can be an expensive business.

The Millionaire

Paris was on the phone. The strong French accent of a lawyer sought my help. His client was being mercilessly defamed in a publication circulating worldwide. 'But why ring me in London?', I enquired. 'The journal is printed and published in your city, in England.' Understood. 'Would you come to Paris?' Who could refuse such an offer? 'Certainly, but when?' 'As soon as possible', the voice responded.

I thought about Paris. Had first gone there as a student, rucksack on back. Wandered through France and Italy. Wrote a book, aged 21, about my travels. Returned there a few years later as a lawyer. Conducted an arbitration in halting French. Deceased academicians turned in their graves. Later I visited with my wife. We ate our way through *Michelin*'s starred favourites. Years passed, conferences called, art galleries beckoned, confiseries and pâtisseries dazzled. Paris was always a pleasure, tempting city of all the senses.

We emerged from grey, concrete Charles de Gaulle airport to be met and wafted into town to an immediate meeting with the lawyer's libelled client. I was not prepared for the setting. We entered a cool inner courtyard, climbed some steps, then passed through high impressive wooden doors which opened onto a vast expanse of halls and rooms.

It resembled a small palace. The interior reminded me of the celebrated Wallace Collection in London's West End: classical 18th century furniture, inlaid with pearl and marquetry; china, rare in colour and design, oil paintings framed in gold (or so it seemed); rich sweeping drapes adorning long windows, sofas and settees of damask on carpets of quality; fountains of glistening chandeliers hanging from far-away ceilings. Beyond the windows, an elegant garden provided an inevitable finishing touch.

Lackeys appeared, removed coats, provided refreshments, attended to needs. Soon the owner of all this finery greeted us. His genial informality contrasted with the surroundings; a friendly, cultured man, an Arab, and a devout Christian, as the small chapel in his establishment testified. He guided us from room to room, but it was the chapel, with shining white lilies surrounding a statue of the Virgin, that was his especial pride. Apart from the case, much of our conversation was on religious themes.

Being a man who had based his life on the teachings of his faith, (apart from Jesus's advice to the rich young man to sell all his worldly goods), he was profoundly shocked at the wicked campaign of vilification pursued against him, week after week, in this widely-read journal. He was well-known in scientific, educational, and religious circles. His reputation was being ruined by the endless libels. He could not allow it to continue. Something had to be done.

At first the articles did not refer to him by name. The editor, gaining confidence, then began to use his initials. Eventually, in the absence of any reaction, the client was mentioned by name. The editor told him there would be no pause in the war of defamation until certain payments were made.

The good Christian finally decided enough was enough. Criminal libel proceedings were taken in France. I explained this was not possible in London, but as the journal was printed and published in England, we could ask the English civil courts to put a stop to this terrible war of defamation.

I was shown a selection of journals printed in Arabic. The contents were translated. Libel was heaped upon libel, untruth upon untruth – drug smuggler's son, associate of drug smugglers, under suspicion by police, investigated by security services, hiding ill-gotten funds, dishonesty, misappropriatation of moneys, illiterate, user of false names, deported from countries, drug-dealer – until the imagination of the editor came to a halt. I was surprised murder, rape, treason, and piracy had not been thrown in. It was appalling. The worst I had ever seen. The man on the Clapham omnibus would have been shocked. I said farewell to client, lawyer and Paris, passionately determined to end this vilification.

Back in London we set to work. Writs, affidavits, court hearings, interim injunctions, all followed. Printers and distributors protested, tried to make amends (the Defamation Act, 1952, helped innocent parties), but the court would not listen. There was nothing innocent. It looked like malice galore; not a single issue but an avalanche of vicious typescript and print. The court felt as strongly as I did.

The case followed the usual legal processes. Documents were exchanged, parties swore to high heaven which documents they had, which ones they used to have, which ones they intended to keep close to their chests, far away from the greedy eyes of their opponents. This is a procedure known as 'discovery of documents' – curious use of the word 'discovery'. Often, in this process, all kinds of golden nuggets are revealed and runaway litigants are brought up with a jolt.

We continued famously on our way, overcoming all legal obstacles, getting orders, injunctions, even judgements when the adversary failed to comply with the orders. One defendant was on the point of paying a sum loaded with noughts to extricate themselves, when suddenly we too were brought up with a jolt.

Our devout client had meant what he had said: he had just wanted his good name cleared and restored. Money was of no interest to him. A jury might have awarded him hundreds of thousands of pounds: he was not interested. There was an apology, bold and clear, on the front cover of the next issue. Readers throughout the world could read the journal's deep regret and of the client's uprightness, all there in print. The journal bowed its head, agreed never again to repeat the operation. Not a single lying sentence. Ever.

A good name had been stolen and restored, as far as it could be. Money was of no consequence. Lawyers in our office were pictures of frustration. Rarely would there be such a clear-cut case, such clear-cut damages – ordinary, aggravated, exemplary. But, as I pointed out, rarely would there be such a man as our Parisian client. All he ever wanted was to clear his name. This he achieved. Money mattered not at all. Rare case. Rare, rare man.

Chapter XIV

Tamil Times

Introduction

The world is full of minorities. Every time a country becomes independent, a new minority is born. Nowhere was this seen more clearly than in the Commonwealth of Independent States following the dissolution of the Soviet Union. There is barely a European country without a minority. The same applies on other continents.

It is not easy to be a minority. It takes time to learn. My own Jewish ancestors have had experience since the days of the Egyptian Pharaohs. Not that others need such a long time, or can afford to wait millennia.

The secret of minority survival seems to be twofold. First, to have a state where there is a reasonable degree of tolerance. Spain under Isabella in 1492 was intolerant. The Turkish rulers of that time were tolerant. Jews who had been evicted from Spain found a haven and lived in peace for hundreds of years in the Turkish domain.

The second requirement is for a minority not to be seen as a threat to the established order, and to respect the ways of the majority. How many minorities have still not learned this crucial lesson. If a minority keeps calling the majority racist, that is how the majority may well finish up. Generally, minorities taking riotously to the streets, or committing acts of violence, deepen majority hostility.

The island of Sri Lanka (formerly Ceylon) just south of India is, I am told, beautiful. It is known for its tea, its beaches, its scenic hills, as the home of science-fiction writer Arthur C. Clarke, and for having the world's first woman prime minister. The largest minority, about 20% of the population, are Tamils, who are mostly Hindus. The majority, about 75%, are Sinhalese, who are mainly Buddhists.

Both communities were founded long ago by invaders from India. For hundreds of years there had been a Tamil kingdom in the north and a Sinhalese kingdom in the south. There were other, later, invaders. The Portuguese arrived in the 16th century, followed by the Dutch a century later. The British came in 1796 and remained in control until independence in 1948.

My first contact with the Tamils was to advise on an agreement for the digging of water holes in the north of the island. Although many rivers flow down from the central mountains, through forests, tea and rubber plantations, to the coastal plain, there are areas that depend on irrigation and the search for water. There were not many precedents about water holes in the law books, but it gave me an insight into some of the problems of the Tamils.

They live largely in the north, around Jaffna, and along the east coast, although they can also be found in other parts, including the capital Colombo. They often hold offices of importance, but complain about being passed over for jobs, the failure to respect the Tamil language (especially in official Government quarters), the neglect of Tamil areas, and the diversion of much needed resources away from their region.

There had been trouble in the 1940s over the language issue, when the majority proposed making Sinhala the official language. There were further riots in 1958 after that proposal became law.

Trouble often erupts from a feeling of discrimination and injustice, yet one section of the Tamils have lived on the island for 2000 years: they are no new minority. They have a rich culture, and culture so often finds its living expression in language.

In 1983, an eruption took place between the main minority and majority populations. The consequences of that eruption still reverberate in the exotic palm-fringed island. I found myself, in that year, playing a role in London that initially had nothing to do with my legal qualification or practice, but which gave me an insight into another of Britain's many minorities, a gifted one, of whom I had previously known nothing.

The Story

An organisation I sometimes advised was the Association of Commonwealth Teachers, which represented the interests of many overseas teachers who helped to fill gaps in Britain's educational system. It was run largely by Jayam Thamotheram, a Tamil from Sri Lanka and senior mathematics teacher in one of London's finest schools. We became good friends. We visited each other's homes. I attended Tamil weddings and, curiously, brought greetings from Jewish bodies, like the Board of Deputies, to Tamil gatherings.

I got to know this peaceful, courteous, exceptionally gifted and highly qualified community: surgeons, professors, scientists, as well as businessmen and women. I was impressed. They were especially proud of their library in Jaffna, which contained a vast quantity of books. Perhaps because they were also a people of the book, I had a special sympathy for them.

I confess, however, that because of my links, I heard only of Tamil grievances. I had little idea of any alternative viewpoint. Then came one of those volcanic social upheavals that devastate civilised society and set the tone for decades, if not centuries.

What amounted to a mass pogrom took place. Tamils were slaughtered by the hundreds. Tens of thousands of their shops and homes were destroyed. Refugees fled to the hills, to the north, wherever they could find safety in numbers. Their great pride, the Jaffna library, was set on fire and destroyed. It was as if a people's culture was being annihilated. Tamils the world over – in Australia, the United States, Singapore, not least in Britain – were horrified. A leading Tamil academic stated, 'About 100,000 priceless works – most of them irreplaceable – went up in flames. For Tamils it was an act of destruction comparable to the torching of the great library of Alexandria.'

Behind the rioting, looting, burning and killing was the basic desire of the Tamils to control their own destiny, even to have a state of their own. Both Tamils and Sinhalese died in the outburst of hate. The Sri Lankan Parliament outlawed any group advocating a separate Tamil state.

My friend Jayam – Tam as I called him – asked me to help his community and organise a protest that would rouse the people of Britain – no easy task. The mass of the British population, apart from religious welfare bodies and pioneering individuals, are rarely roused except through a major media campaign. In the late 1980s and early 1990s thousands of Christians perished in Sudan, and 100,000 died the previous decade in Lebanon, with not the slightest sign of mass concern in Britain. The media were not interested, so the public were not roused.

Iraq, with perhaps the worst human rights record in the world, only became objectionable when it invaded Kuwait in 1990, threatening Western interests. The fact that thousands had been brutally annihilated, even gassed to death, at the hands of that detestable regime throughout the 1980s in no way prevented British arms and supplies pouring into the country, even as late as 1990.

Tam therefore faced a huge task in mobilising public opinion. Sri Lanka was a far-off island. Few knew it, few cared about it. The British had trouble enough with endless violence in Northern Ireland, based on similar ethnic and religious differences.

I was asked not for legal advice, but for public relations advice. What was proposed was a major march and demonstration down Whitehall, and the presentation of a petition to the Prime Minister at 10 Downing Street. Also proposed was the establishment of a Tamil emergency committee, the sending of relief supplies, food, clothing and other urgently-needed items to Sri Lanka, opening a headquarters office, holding a press conference, and approaching all branches of the media to publicise the plight of the Tamils in their island home.

It was a tall order, but I managed to help. I found an office for them, and organised a press conference. Relief supplies were collected and despatched, the march took place (duly recorded by television), and releases were issued to the press. At the same time it was decided to establish a journal in which the Tamil case could be presented to the world. My sole contribution to that newspaper was to suggest its title, *The Tamil Times*. That remains its title.

The most revealing episode for me was the setting up of the Tamil Emergency Committee, representing all branches of the community. I was asked to find a suitable venue and chose the National Liberal Club, where, in earlier days, I used to play snooker in the marvellous basement, long since transformed.

We gathered one afternoon, some 40 or more Tamils representing all their major bodies and organisations in Britain. I was asked to chair the meeting.

I have found myself in many anomalous situations in my life, but this was one of the most extraordinary – 40 Tamils with a Jewish chairman. It was an honour, and a revelation. What I detected then were attitudes and divisions that later came to the fore and affected the Tamil cause. The majority were concerned with the relief of suffering and mobilising public opinion, but a small group of hawks clearly gave priority to the supply of arms for self-defence and the establishment of a military force.

It was the belief of the latter group – that a minority had to defend itself militarily – which led to the creation of the Tamil Tigers, and a reign of violence during the ensuing decade. With this came a demand for Elam, an independent state in the north and east. The fiercer the Tigers tore at the army and the institutions of state, the more determined were the authorities not to surrender to what they regarded as a form of terrorism. Many hundreds of innocent people continued to lose their lives. Many fled to Britain and elsewhere.

In the House of Commons, the Home Secretary announced a special status for the Tamils who fled here. They were to be allowed to stay for a period, but not to have the status either of immigrants or political refugees.

Tamils sought my advice. Many wanted to stay in Britain, professional people who would be a great asset to the country. Could they prove a real fear of persecution if returned home? It was not easy. In many countries, the laws, or absence of laws, the reigns of terror, the political incarceration, torture and death, were well-documented.

That was not so easy with the Tamils, as confused messages were coming from different parts of the country, and from British diplomatic offices. Whoever came would be leaving one minority status for another. It was not easy to convince the Home Office, who were facing the problem of the sudden descent of refugees from different parts of the world, all claiming political asylum.

Years later I heard the Sinhalese version of what had happened in 1983 and since. Needless to say, it bore little relation to the view with which I was most familiar. The plight of the Tamils is yet one more sad chapter in the agonised march of the 20th century; in the failure of majority and minority to show tolerance, to adapt and to adjust.

Apart from problems of the environment and of hunger, the world's greatest problem remains that of group relations.

It is loyalty to the group that gives security and identity. It is also loyalty to the group, as opposed to universal human values, that leads to disaster. It is an extraordinarily complex problem, one mankind has not been able to solve since the beginning of our recorded existence.

If we managed to solve it, it would represent the dawn of a new age and a new man, a new heaven, and a new earth. Until that day we have to struggle with what we have, as we painfully evolve towards tolerance and a society in which man's worst instincts can be channelled into civilised and peaceful avenues. The Tamil saga goes on, one more episode in a never-ending process of moral and human evolution. The tensions and killings continue, year after year. A beautiful land is stained by the ugliness in the human soul.

Thus I had the pleasure of learning about their ancient culture of which I had previously known nothing: a culture that had produced learned writers and thinkers of high intelligence. Culture depends on communication, and communication depends on language. One can perceive, therefore, the fear of the Tamil minority when the survival of their language appeared to be threatened, although in recent years progress has been made in recognising their language nationally.

Fear inevitably leads to violence. Whether the violence that ensued in Sri Lanka from the 1980s, and continued into the 1990s, will achieve anything positive remains to be seen. I have my doubts. Elam seems further away than ever. Both minority and majority have still to learn the lesson of history.

Chapter XV

The Expert Witness

Introduction

It was a warm summer's day in 1992. My wife and I, after much walking, sat ourselves thankfully down at a table set out on the lawn. There were many such tables, many such lawns. We had been wandering in the capacious grounds behind Buckingham Palace, two of the many thousands who annually attend garden parties graciously given by the Queen.

I looked at the distinguished woman sitting with her husband across the table from us. Her name was Rose Heilbron, a famous legal name, one of the first women to become a QC and, later, a high court judge; a woman who retained not only her mental alertness and supreme self-possession, but also her cordiality and her looks.

I had briefed her many decades before. Our paths had never crossed since. She could not recall the case. It revolved around a very young child and the failure of hospital experts to diagnose a congenital malformation of the hip. By the time a correct diagnosis had been made, it was too late to take the necessary remedial action. The child would be crippled for life. Were the experts negligent or did they have legitimate and justifiable doubts as to the nature of the child's disability? No easy answer.

I recalled the case for several reasons. One was the quality of the barrister, Rose Heilbron; the second was a weighty text-book on orthopaedics which I assiduously studied from beginning to end; the third, the difficult burden of anyone holding him or herself out as an expert.

Medical negligence cases, which have boomed and so bedevilled medical practice in Britain, but more particularly in writ-happy United States, were few in number in those days. Negligence is a breach of duty to take care. That duty is heightened when one holds out special knowledge, qualifications, or expert ability.

Yet the expert is human, fallible. Experts of one generation are not the same as those of another. Knowledge, experience, discoveries, move on, ever faster.

Over the years, my heart has gone out to the expert witness; whether for or against me. An expert's whole career and reputation can be destroyed by a subtle and searching cross-examination. i recall to mind one such case.

Chicken had once been a luxury for many families. The arrival of the intensive system of breeding and raising them heralded an eating revolution. Chicken became available for all, and at a reasonable price.

Mass consumption depended on mass production. The chickens entered enormous deep litter houses, where they were scientifically watered, fed, cleaned, heated, and ventilated. Conditions were abnormal. A glance into a deep litter house – never to my taste – reminded me of Wordsworth's line, 'Ten thousand saw I at a glance'. But a very special kind of poultry husbandry was necessary, especially in those early days, for birds to remain healthy and alive, and for production to stay profitable.

A leading manufacturer of deep litter poultry houses was being sued by a poultry farmer for the loss of thousands of young chickens, and so sought my help. The claim asserted that the ventilation of the building was defective, and, as a result, the poor birds in those cavernous timber buildings were perishing at an alarming rate, far above the anticipated 6 or 7%. The farmer was indignant. He claimed substantial compensation.

The defence amounted to an attack on the farmer's competence. Dealing with an intensive system of poultry production demanded experience and expertise. In any event, the same building, with the same ventilation, was in successful operation up and down the country, without undue loss of birds.

Thus was battle joined before a judicial officer known as an Official Referee. Today the press would regard him in footballing terms. The principal witness for the claimant was an expert in ventilation; top of his field at university, adviser emeritus to industry, initials galore following his name. But of appearance in witness boxes, he appeared to know nothing.

I agonised for him as our counsel, combative, assertive, perceptive, launched into the poor man. Within three hours the expert's credibility had been destroyed, and the claim lay in legal tatters.

My sympathy went to the expert. He had not appreciated that a court is sometimes a battlefield. His attempts to be fair, resolve inconsistencies, enlarge on scientific detail, were suited to the tutorial and the consultant's office, not the thrust of pointed questions and experienced advocacy.

I recall the case for two reasons. One was the terrible danger to which a self-proclaimed expert is exposed when a tigerish counsel is on the prowl. The other was the name of the claimant, Horatio Nelson; a name I found difficult to relate to chicken farming.

In the practice of the law we recruit the aid of experts constantly. How often did I involve handwriting experts where wills and documents were alleged to have been forged. Fingerprint evidence also produced conflicts of views. The geography of a print gave rise to a variation of expert comments. Also, in claims for damages when people were injured, both sides garnered expert reports on vehicles, on industrial processes, on resulting health problems. It was remarkable how often reports differed, dependent on the side the expert was advising.

One unusual case intrigued me. A consultant gave his expert prognosis as to how long it would take for a patient to recover from a whiplash injury sustained in a car accident. A year or more was mentioned. On that basis, an insurance company paid over a sum of money. Within weeks the injured party had seen a healer, whose hands somehow overrode medical forecasts, and the effects of the injury disappeared.

I pondered how much insurers could save if they employed a panel of such healers. However, I did not think they would give credence to such a novel suggestion and abandoned the idea of writing to them. Yet something new and unforeseen had intervened outside the contemplation of the expert, who rightly operated within the parameters of accepted professional wisdom.

Whilst I sympathise with experts when exposed to rigorous questioning, I have never had blind faith in their opinion. I have always put other possibilities, or consequences, to them.

The building and construction world is full of arguments, arbitrations, notices, claims. Were the plans awry or the builders deficient? Call in the experts. The experts often called in further experts. It can be an expensive business for laymen and litigants. Deficiencies of the double glazing world have spawned cases galore, and the inevitable experts. I had a certain caution about experts. I recall the painter-forger Van Mergeren, who for years fooled all the art experts.

Whatever the courts may say, expertise inevitably remains subjective, tinctured with a touch of pride, though usually also with professional sincerity.

There is a much more serious side to the expert witness. 1992 saw a flurry of appeals where men and women, imprisoned for years on the basis of expert evidence, were released. The evidence was challenged, and proved to be suspect. The prisoners had to be released, said the Court of Appeal. It was unsafe to let the convictions stand. The whole question of expert scientific evidence was thrown into doubt.

This has led to talk of an independent forensic service. Former methods of chemical testing, once accepted as unchallengeable, were challenged and proved to be less than certain – no basis for a long prison sentence.

Even at the time of penning these lines, I am investigating the whole system of identifying DNA. Scientific evidence, accepted by the British courts, and now rejected by the American courts, has resulted in a young man spending years in jail for a crime I am convinced he did not commit.

But to persuade the Home Office and the Court of Appeal to re-open enquiries or grant an appeal is no easy matter, and, in my present case, we are at the start of a complicated scientific journey, where self-interest and commercial interest may well vie with the need for overwhelming forensic accuracy.

We pursue justice in practising the law. Prolonged injustice can lead to a disturbed society. It is for the good of all that justice, or as near to justice as we can get, is our goal. The expert can be a partner in that objective, but never an arbiter of the cause.

When experts comment on the state of a person's mind, rather than the body, the problem becomes more uncertain, and the consequences even more so, a point aptly illustrated in the story that follows.

The Story

There was no doubt he had killed his wife. The question was, did he murder her? The further, more significant question, was whether he knew what he was doing at the time, and, if he did, whether he knew his action was wrong.

I sat in the cell with him in a dreary provincial prison. Abraham and Moses were there with us, he told me. Not only these Biblical figures, but also the Virgin Mary and St. Teresa (dressed normally) and Pope Paul (in special papal vestments). A short time later, however, he was able to talk rationally about his history, and a short and chequered one it proved to be.

He was unloved by his father, who beat his mother. His parents divorced. His mother tried to kill herself. He found himself with a stepfather and a stepmother. His stepfather committed suicide. His own young wife tried to commit suicide. Enough to unhinge the mind of any young man.

Yet somehow he had spent a few happy and useful years in the Royal Air Force, then found a job as a lathe turner after a training-centre course. He found a wife, a registered nurse, whom he married. Accommodation was limited in London, so they moved to a country town. He obtained employment there. His wife couldn't. It was lonely away from his friends.

On a cold November morning he arrived at a London railway terminus. He rang the police station in his home town. He told them to send an ambulance to his address, mentioning an attempted suicide. He wanted someone to find his wife's body. He did not want it to rot. He rang again. He told the police he had killed his wife. They kept him talking while local London officers sped to the telephone booth, where they arrested him.

Sitting in the gloomy prison cell, the story emerged. He had been brought up strictly as a Roman Catholic. He had had visions. He had been treated by a psychiatrist – pills and electric shocks. He saw red marks on people's foreheads. He was the dead body of Che Guevara. A voodoo cult were after him.

On the day he killed his wife, he had, in the morning, seen the markings again. People were coming to mutilate his body and throw him into a swamp. He saw the faces of the potential attackers. His body was going to be used as a sacrifice by the Roman Catholic Church. Though distraught with these visions, he went to work, returning home at 6.00 p.m.

He had another fear. The assailants were about to put him in a zoo, take his wife away from him, and give her to a friend of his, whom he named. He agreed his wife, who was three months pregnant, had never mentioned leaving him. Suddenly, an hour after he had returned home, he again saw the people coming to chop him up. He did not want his wife to see him in such a condition. He would end his wife's life and then commit suicide. She could not then leave him for his friend. The Pope confirmed he would be mutilated. He saw the people moving forward to attack him, destroy him, tear him to pieces.

He picked up a kitchen knife and stabbed his wife in the throat, the neck, the abdomen. It happened suddenly. She fell to the ground without a word. Blood was everywhere. He had to make sure she was dead before he was chopped up. She must not see him mutilated. He choked her round the neck, and also with a pillow case. He was still ashamed lest she saw him cut to pieces. He drowned her in the bath, let the water out, and cleaned the room.

The television had been on all the while. His wife used to watch whilst knitting clothes for their expected baby. He laid his dead wife on the bed, placed a crucifix and four wedding rings on the body. The people were coming to attack him. He left the house hurriedly, thought of ways of committing suicide, returned to the house, and sat there all night.

Next morning he left early, before the religious groups and the Catholic Church caught up with him. He found himself eventually at Kings Cross Station, from where he rang the police.

We sat quietly in the cell. He talked quietly, this young man, short in stature, of pallid complexion beneath carefully combed black hair. He told me of his visions, his fears. They surrounded him. They possessed him. He felt as if he were programmed, as if a hex had been put on him.

He had once, through jealousy, thrown boiling water over his wife. He had had a vision with markings showing his marriage had been annulled. Voices had said he was part of an experiment with radio waves. Above all he was in constant fear of snakes, and of being consigned to a snake pit. He mentioned films he had seen: *The Exorcist, The Snake Pit.*

Coincidentally, not long before this interview, a Christian author had given me a copy of his own work, *The Exorcist and the Possessed.* I re-read it with renewed interest. Possession was bound up with a sense of sin. A distinct force of evil was overcome only by good, by faith, by religion. The author had conducted 2000 exorcisms. Those afflicted often needed a minister of religion, rather than a psychiatrist.

Awareness of evil spirits often brought awareness of the Holy Spirit.

The already disturbed mind of the man sitting with me in the cell had somehow incorporated into his visions the graphic and vivid scenes he had witnessed in the two films.

I left him, saddened at the events, and at the pathos of a brain that had lost its balance.

With the police, I wandered around his silent, unprepossessing home, with its clothes and books, record player and television set. The house was part of an anonymous council estate, isolated, on the edge of a field with trees behind. The prisoner had seen the attackers coming at him from the trees.

How the world had changed suddenly for that young couple. They had lived there, day after day, she knitting clothes, he earning a weekly wage. A baby was expected. It could have been the start of a happy life. Yet something in his brain, his mind, his soul, had snapped. The wife was dead. No baby would see the light of day. He was in prison awaiting trial.

He pleaded not guilty to the murder charge but guilty of manslaughter. It was agreed on both sides that it was a case of diminished responsibility. Eminently so, commented the judge. That was the only matter on which the parties agreed. If the defendant was guilty of manslaughter, what was to be done with him?

The judge found himself faced with a bevy of experts, all highly qualified psychiatrists, all with a string of impressive initials, all in total disagreement. Three of them asserted that, at the time of the killings and subsequently, the young husband suffered from a personality disorder, and should be sent to prison.

Two equally distinguished experts, with the backing of several others not present in court, disagreed. The prisoner was not suffering from a personality disorder, but from paranoid schizophrenia. He should not be sent to prison. A hospital bed was the correct destination for him, in an approved establishment.

The poor judge was also disturbed, though not to the extent of the prisoner. He expressed his perplexity:

'A most unusual situation has arisen in this case. Three consultant psychiatrists have come to one conclusion, and two equally eminent consultant psychiatrists have come to the opposite conclusion.'

What should he do? He could have tossed a coin, and either way he would have had expert backing for his decision. He reviewed the evidence set out in written reports, and confirmed in the witness box. What follows is a summary of expert opinions.

Expert number one: 'A man of markedly abnormal personality, poorly integrated and weakly controlled personality, no psychotic illness, preoccupied with fears, incorporating the need for exorcising himself of some devil, high degree of impulsivity, no evidence of a true psychotic thought disorder incorporating valid hallucinating material which would substantiate a diagnosis of formal thought disorder, a disturbed personality under stress, no disease of the mind at the time of the killing, but an abnormality amounting to a substantial diminution of responsibility arising from inherent causes within the terms of the Homicide Act, 1957. No paranoid schizophrenia.'

Hence no bed, under the Mental Health Act, 1959, no mental hospital, no special hospital.

Expert number two: 'Agreed about the visions. The prisoner saw the Queen and a procession of Saints passing before him. He wanted to be a priest and make his wife a Saint. Low intelligence, some depression, considerable guilt feeling. No evidence of schizophrenic illness, but considerable personality problems.'

Prison and no bed.

Expert number three: 'During a long interview he presented a changing picture, showing no signs of psychosis whatsoever, hysterical, inadequacy, inadequate personality, at present time he is precariously balanced.'

However prison and no bed.

Expert number four (this expert had treated him after the boiling water incident, had had him under observation for weeks in hospital): 'Confirmed details of the visions, hallucinations, and schizophrenia diagnosed by himself and colleagues when prisoner in hospital. Guilty and expectation of punishment there as in all types of demonical possessions. Personality distortion due to a serious mental disorder, not a primary personality disorder. Definitely suffering from paranoid schizophrenia.'

No prison. Bed in a mental hospital with long stay facilities.

Expert number five (by this time I had become accustomed to the jargon of the profession. Number five kept using 'perseverate' which Chambers defines as 'to repeat the same actions or thoughts'. My vocabulary was expanding): 'Personality disorder has several names, equivalent to psychopathic personality, behaviour disorder, or character disorder. The person does not adjust to society, doesn't learn from experience. Paranoid schizophrenia is a mental disease of no known origin. There are many theories. It is a disorder of all functions of the brain and the mind, of the feeling, thinking, and behaving. It can go on for life, changing from time to time. No point sending him to prison. Section 72 of the Act says if ill he can go into hospital, then when better, back to prison, no point in this. Section 60 should apply. Definitely paranoid schizophrenia.'

Bed and no prison.

Expert number one was recalled. He differed fundamentally with number five. In his view: 'Psychiatry is bedevilled by semantics. People put different interpretations upon different words, there are various degrees of paranoia.'

I was by this time experiencing a mild degree of paranoia myself. Number one stuck to his guns. Definitely a personality disorder – prison.

What could the judge do? Personality disorder was beating paranoid schizophrenia by three to two. He ruled, 'I am not satisfied that this defendant is suffering from paranoid schizophrenia', and sentenced him to life imprisonment.

The Defendant was addressed by the judge. 'Diminished responsibility. You need treatment for your depression and personality problems.' The prisoner must have been in a greater daze than the rest of us. The experts had spoken, with forked tongues.

Numbers four and five were shocked. Subsequent reports flowed in, commenting on the evidence and the judge's predicament in the face of 'such a great difference of opinion among expert witnesses'.

Mention was made of an assessment by an independent university forensic department. This proved unnecessary.

We lodged an appeal against sentence, produced further evidence, especially that of the prison's medical officers. They had watched the prisoner's behaviour for eight months – his attempted jump from a top floor landing, the continuous hallucinations. The Holy Family were now in his cell controlling his mind.

They decided to call in expert number six, who agreed with four and five, which, added to the weight of the prison medical officers and the availability of a hospital bed, induced the Court of Appeal to remove him from prison. Section 60 was in, life imprisonment out.

This poor unfortunate man had spent over a year in prison before his appeal could be heard. Perhaps prison or hospital may not have made much difference to what was going on within his tormented brain.

Perhaps the language of the experts, and their contradictory opinions, meant nothing to him. He bore his own sense of guilt, of fear, of living in a minatory world, where the ubiquitous 'they' were out to get him. He expressed his relief that he had got his wife away from the priests. He still thought his only end would be as a human sacrifice.

Yet he was one of us: a human being, with, somewhere, a spark of the divine within him. He had taken the life of his wife. Number five later told me that, in his mental state, he would have taken the life of any future wife he might have had.

Did we, concerned society, deal with him in the best way? Are the courts still the best venue for assessing the mental condition of an accused person? I would have liked to have placed numbers one to five in a room and let them debate the matter exhaustively, then emerge with an agreed decision, or, failing that, their reasons for disagreement. And what does it say of expertise when eminent opinion can differ so profoundly? How far is it hit and miss? How far subjective? How far an indication that psychiatry is as much an art as a science?

The young man remained in hospital. His father, incidentally, in another country, was Chief Public Prosecutor – of people who committed murder or manslaughter, whatever their state of mind.

The father felt we had done all that was possible. I felt so too, but I felt deeply for the wife, cut off so tragically in her short life; for the unborn child; for the man himself, living in his tortured world; and for the world of laws and experts in which he was engulfed.

Chapter XVI

Hallelujah! Praise the Lord!

Introduction

There are certain peoples who have a natural feel for religion. Whilst all people try to explain the unknown, propitiate the unknown out of fear, or dedicate themselves to the unknown out of love, it would not be unfair to say that the main faiths of the world ultimately emanated from two peoples – the Jews and the Indians. Much is dissimilar in the beliefs flowing from these two streams, but both took over primitive practices and raised them to universal meaning by the sublimity of their moral teachings. Both used all the senses in the service of prayers, and both tried to explore the inner and future condition of each individual soul.

Out of the Vedas and Upanishads and the Hindu tradition developed, each in its own special way, Buddhism, Jainism, Sikhism, whilst out of the books of Moses and the Hebrew prophets developed Christianity and Islam and offshoots of those remarkable faiths. And, in the modern development of Christianity, a fascinating phenomenon has emerged, namely the black Christian churches, whose members and adherents are largely of African and Afro-Caribbean background.

The figure of Jesus, as one who overcame suffering, was identified as a beacon of hope by the enslaved black peoples of Africa, the West Indies and the United States.

Cruelly treated by the dominant white Europeans and colonialists, they identified with the Hebrew slaves of the Egyptian Pharaoh. They looked to the divine power to help them through the travails of this life, and a hoped-for future across the symbolic river Jordan. They found great inspiration in the New Testament. They sang spirituals expressing profound faith, love and yearning. They established churches and communities in many countries, bringing great fervour to the sermon, the music, the prayers, and a desire to express their uplifting faith in words and music, rhythmically, boldly, happily.

For some years, leaders of the black churches in Britain and I had had a happy dialogue. But in the early summer of 1991, I found myself in one of those anomalous situations which follow me from year to year, and to which I was becoming accustomed, though perplexed.

At the very same time as being nominated for the office of vice-president of the Board of Deputies of British Jews, the body representing over 300,000 Jews in Britain (an office I subsequently held), I was invited by the bishops and pastors of the New Assembly of Churches, representing a similar number of Christians and their families, to become their president.

It was an extraordinary proposal. I had, in my capacity as a lawyer, created a legal structure for the New Assembly of Churches, and, as a result, had had many meetings with their leaders, but to be asked to head their organisation was overwhelming. It invoked in me all kinds of reaction: amazement, humility, a great fellow-feeling. My thoughts centred on the Jewish religious bodies I knew, and the unlikely event of a black Christian becoming their president.

I explained to the Church leaders that I was moved and honoured by their invitation, but that a church body had to have a true Christian, and not a Jew, at its head. They understood. They asked, however, if I would be their Patron. I agreed. From that date I have been closely identified with their work, chairing meetings, advising individual churches, even speaking in the churches. From 1993 I was honoured to have the Archbishop of Canterbury, Dr George Carey, as my co-Patron.

These churches are a major force, indeed an avenue of hope, in the black community in Britain. Most of the members emanate from the West Indies, but there are those from other backgrounds who attend. They do important pastoral work, especially among their young people, many of whom find themselves in conflict with the law and their own families. They visit prisons, find jobs, above all give a sense of dignity and identity to a minority who have had considerable problems in adjusting to the values and conventions of the white majority, as well as being overtaken in economic progress by a number of Britain's other minorities.

One of my greatest pleasures is to be invited to their churches, often as a visitor, occasionally as a preacher. The latter is a rare experience. I have, in the subsequent light-hearted account (which I hope my black colleagues will not take amiss), tried to convey the happiness and fun, sense of community and devotion of one such service.

If ever the words 'Make a joyful noise unto the Lord' meant anything, they find their reality in the lively and expanding black churches of Britain.

The Story

The black pastor welcomed me with warmth and sincerity, saying how pleased he was that I had agreed to preach the sermon that day. His Church of God, basically Afro-Caribbean in membership with branches in Jamaica, Barbados, Nigeria, and, surprisingly, Egypt, was celebrating its 25th anniversary.

In the main hall, noticeably free of any statue, painting, or religious representation, groups of young men and women were engaged in Bible study. In rooms above, children's religious classes were in progress. Babies, old people, choristers in blue dresses and white blouses, were assembling, neatly, smartly dressed. This was an occasion.

In his office, the pastor told us of his regard for the Jewish people, for Israel, for the heroic figures of the Old Testament. A Magen David (Shield of David emblem) hung from the wall, but no human representation. Others joined us; the pastor's svelte and smiling wife; another visiting minister and general secretary of the New Assembly of Churches, the national umbrella body of twelve churches in which each church had many congregations, teachers and leaders of local communities. The general secretary confirmed to me that his organisation encompassed over 300,000 souls including members and their families.

We stood in a circle in the minister's room and, as is their custom, held hands. Each uttered prayers in his or her own words at variable speeds, a babble of conflicting voices, like a Jewish committee meeting, but with a sense of awe, eyes tightly closed.

We then entered the packed church. The congregation were dressed in their smartest clothes. I was invited to sit on the platform with the ministers. Behind us stood a choir, 25 strong, mainly women. Below at the side sat an organist, prim, proper, in dark suit, white blouse, perky white hat. All the women wore hats.

The minister – slow-speaking, sincere, dignified – welcomed us (my wife and me), and gave thanks for 25 years of service and services. A visiting minister gave the invocation. All was spontaneous, nothing written, no notes, all natural, alive, as the spirit moved. This was no audience, no us-and-them relationship. Bursts of thanks and praise rose from all over the room, punctuating prayers, creating a unity, a communal solidarity.

And O! the music, the singing! Heartwarming, full of rhythm, beat, life. The choir was not for listening to, admiring, as if giving a performance; it led a full-throated mass sound of praise, drowning the organ. And if the spirit moved them, they repeated verses already sung. It was glorious. It was natural. My feet, unobserved, began to tap out the infectious rhythm. It had rarely happened to me in any other house of prayer.

Two great heroes of my late teens and early twenties had been Mahaliah Jackson, the magnificent Southern Baptist black gospel singer, and Mordechai Hershman, a brilliant Jewish cantor. I knew their records by heart, from 'I'm glad salvation is free', to the Jewish prayer for rain. They had much in common. Services, primarily, have to have feeling, not meaning. For meaning you study. Often out of feeling comes meaning.

The minister introduced me to the congregation. 'Mr Rose is a Jew.' Immediately a label, one I was proud to accept. It was a first, for them and for me. Another leader on the platform prayed for me, that I might speak well and have wisdom. He must have known my problems.

I thanked them, congratulated them. I was honoured. I understood how they, as immigrants, had met coldness from people who did not understand the heart of the stranger (communal nodding of heads, shouts of 'Yes, yes'), but they had overcome problems (excitement, exclamations of 'Hallelujah, praise the Lord'), they would continue to overcome problems, (increased excitement, 'Yes, yes' and 'Yes Lord, praise be!', from all sides).

I compared Easter and Passover, quoted the teaching of the Rabbi from Galilee, related how Moses had spoken to Pharaoh as an equal and told him (the entire congregation in unison, before I could finish the sentence - 'Let my people go'). I kept a straight face. Those words, I explained, had inspired the Negro slaves, as well as tormented Jews in the racist Soviet Union.

But the Israelites had to throw off the mentality of servants. This took 40 years, but it happened, and the people crossed over ('Yes,

Lord!') into the Promised Land ('Hallelujah', 'Yes, yes, Lord', 'Crossed over', 'Praise the Lord!').

I quoted extensively from ancient Jewish sources; from the Ethics of the Fathers, Rabbis Hillel, Gamaliel, and ben Zoma. The quotation that struck the deepest chord was from Rabbi Akavya ben Mahalalel. If Akavya, a Talmudic rabbi of old, could have known to whom his words meant so much on that day, he would, I am sure, have been enthralled. He used to say, 'Think on three things to avoid the power of sin: where you have come from, where you are going to, and before whom you will one day give an account and reckoning' (great shouts of agreement and recognition of truth). The visiting minister behind me was moved. He made me repeat the whole quotation. Akavya became a hero of the New Assembly of Churches.

I referred to the Psalms – sing unto the Lord a new song (they knew all the Psalms). I ended with the quotation about how good it was for brothers to dwell together in unity. The congregation finished it for me (shouts of 'Hallelujah', 'Praise the Lord', clapping). I wiped my brow and sat down.

I had conducted services and given sermons in synagogues but I had never before experienced such a lightness of heart, such a sense of communal joy. It reminded me of stories of the 18th century Chasidic movement, whose informality in song and dance is now ossified in the formal patterns of prayer of modern establishments.

We prayed for all those who were ill and anxious and needed to be healed. Not just a few sentences, but an actual physical act of prayer. Everyone bowed down on the ground, on hands and knees, and raised up voices, calling for a complete healing for many people; a hundred individual spontaneous prayers, a Babel of requests, from the heart, as well as the mind. Not only a cerebral invocation, but an emotional outburst. It would never have done at the Church of England. It is something most orthodoxies have recognised, this appeal to all the senses, something they have sometimes used, and abused, but have today largely forgotten.

We left before the service ended. It had begun half an hour late. It was clearly going on and on. The minister thanked me. His wife gave my wife and myself a gift of cake, excellent rum-drenched cake, which sustained us on our journey home. I recalled an old Jewish prayer and blessed the Lord who had preserved me, and kept me alive to take part in such an extraordinary day. Praise be the Lord! Hallelujah!

Chapter XVII

Inshallah

or *How to Steal Forty Million Pounds*

Introduction

E arly in the 1980s, age of materialism *par excellence* in the West, I hired a car in Boston and drove 3,500 miles through half a dozen states in eastern America. The car was built like a fortress, a chariot. When after a day, a problem arose with a tyre, the hire company changed not the tyre, but the car, for an even larger, thirstier chariot.

In this extraordinary vehicle, with wife and daughter, I surveyed the beauties of nature in russet New England, surprising vineyards and Finger Lakes in New York State, magnificent gardens in Delaware and district, Jefferson's stately University of Virginia in Charlottesville, product of the age and sage of reason, and offices of lawyers, rabbis, and a few of the numerous Jewish organisations within that equally extraordinary community.

Visits to the latter derived from my communal work in London for the Board of Deputies of British Jews, founded, incidentally, in 1760, well before the United States came into being.

Whichever office I visited, I was intrigued by the American love of framed diplomas. From pleasant Wilmington to the maelstrom of New York, as I sat talking, my eyes were often diverted from the person with whom I was conversing, to the wall behind. This was invariably smothered with important-looking framed documents, on which illegible signatures set above impressive seals confirmed that the named person possessed a degree or diploma, was admitted to an important professional body, had graduated *cum laude* of some sort, had walked a hundred miles for a worthy cause, had sneezed 12 times consecutively without collapsing, had remained married for at least two years to the same spouse. I resolved that if ever I settled in that country, I would become a framemaker, thus assuring myself of an income for life.

I thought about my office wall in London on which hung, apologetically, a few framed documents, mainly one in which the Law Society (may its memory be remembered for good) held out to the world that I was entitled to continue plying my legal trade. Other certificates slept in filing cabinets, in large, light-brown cardboard envelopes.

And yet, I was the proud owner of one framed document which I doubted any of my transatlantic friends possessed. Printed in green on a white background, in French and Arabic, it confirmed that the Alliance Musulman Universelle had appointed one Aubrey Rose as an ambassador for Islam. Close to the usual scrawled signature was an elaborate embossed motif confirming that Allah was wonderful and Mahomet remained his prophet. That certificate might have puzzled my American friends.

In the late 1970s and early 1980s, Islam awoke in Britain. The poorer, earlier immigrants from Pakistan and Bangladesh now had richer, much richer, co-religionists from Arab lands dwelling in their cities. Oil had moved in, to the delight of Harrods, Rolls-Royce, real estate agents, and expensive five-star hostelries.

Some of the poorer brothers, helped by a few wealthier ones, had been looking for sites for mosques. They had asked my help. I trooped through my old familiar East End, and smart West End, looking at likely prospects, negotiating for some, advising on legal matters, and setting up a charitable foundation, religiously orientated.

We became friends. We met often. Suddenly, in that impulsively-hospitable mood that characterised their world, I found myself invited to Paris, ensconced in a leading hotel (all paid), and, at a ceremony, presented with this fascinating certificate appointing me ambassador for Islam; an office or situation to which I had never aspired and continue to find somewhat incomprehensible. Was I acting out an improbable episode in one of Stephen Leacock's or Spike Milligan's larger lunacies? By this time in my career, however, the unexpected had become expected.

Yet it did happen. I have but to turn my head, and there hangs the green and white certificate, slightly faded, yet living proof that Jews and Muslims can occasionally live peacefully together, have done so in the past, and, inshallah, will do so again in the future.

A subheading for this strange tale could well be the familiar words from the *Book of Psalms*, 'My ways are not your ways, my thoughts are not your thoughts'.

Contact with the world of Islam, and Arabs (the two are not identical), expanded through the decade. We made formal links with Arab lawyers in the Gulf, sent a lawyer there to facilitate affairs to our mutual benefit, even proclaimed on our office notepaper, replete with Jewish names, our associated offices in Sharjah and Abu Dhabi. My partners, long-suffering, were silently convinced of, or at least habituated to, some degree of modified sanity in me, but fortunately never expressed openly their inner doubts. I may have been the senior partner, but they understood that, in my strange antics, I needed a degree of humouring. Their patience was exemplary, and appreciated.

I began to note differences. A prominent Gulf lawyer invited my wife Sheila and me to a restaurant. During the meal, his hand dived into his pocket and emerged with two glittering watches, which he proceeded to present to us as gifts. On my birthday (All Saints Day, linked to Scorpio, with perpetual improbability in the ascendant) there was a knock on my door at home. A messenger delivered a magnificent silver-plated salver, of no mean size, on which rested a veritable mountain of handmade chocolates, adorned with artificial flowers of exquisite colouring and design. Totally unexpected, totally delightful, totally typical. An Arab businessman client was saying something, in his munificent way.

I was frequently a guest at their table at home. Men only sat to eat, half a dozen of us usually, faced with food enough to feed battalions. Hospitality was overwhelming, but women were invisible, never present. This applied to meetings (audiences) I had with one of the Middle Eastern rulers, who had asked me to advise him and his country on a mixture of commercial and financial matters. Again, supreme politeness, exquisite food and drink (always non-alcoholic), great comfort on well-cushioned sofas, yet again no women.

This state of affairs came as a shock to me, as one who feels more at home with women than with men. The burst of unbelieving laughter that erupted when I solemnly stated that I would seek the opinion of my mother-in-law on a particular matter was indicative of their view. Women may not rate high, but mothers-in-law! However, they had not met my mother-in-law, and when they did, they understood better my regard for her.

The Arab and Muslim world has to be understood, appreciated. It is a world of long-established patterns, many centuries old, challenged not only by the modern concept of human rights and equality, but by the sudden impact of vast wealth, untold riches, alongside poverty and illiteracy. Hence the almost love-hate relationship with the West: admiring democracy yet so often incapable of changing government peacefully through the ballot box; seeking new structures and forms, yet interpreting more strictly the Sharia law, where equality between Muslim and non-Muslim does not reign.

I was shocked, on my Paris visit, to hear a cultivated Muslim justify the cutting off of hands as a punishment for theft. Yet I am reminded that it was as recently as the 19th century that English judges were sentencing people to death for the same offence.

But the problems were even more profound. The Arab world, following set patterns for generations, suddenly had to face the immense challenge of the industrial and scientific revolutions. Other lands had adjusted over two centuries: the Arab world had to adjust in decades. Inevitably, these challenges gave rise to progressive and reactionary forces. Everything is still in flux.

Western ideas of human rights and the equality of all men and women, whatever their origin or belief, present the most fundamental challenge to Islam, and to other religions, as equality in Islam was traditionally only accorded to a free Muslim male. Everyone else had a lesser or tolerated status. Hence the ferocity of the reaction and the retreat into what is termed fundamentalism by those who perceive the dire threat of modern concepts, enshrined in declarations and covenants of human rights.

European tyrants and despots of the pre- and post-Reformation period have their Arab counterparts today. When helping to obtain political asylum for prominent Arabs, former ambassadors, army officers, I was amazed at the fear they expressed that their applications should be known by anyone other than myself and the particular Home Office official. They truly believed that the long arm of home tyranny reached into the quietest cloisters of London.

Thus I came upon patterns of life, traditions, views and beliefs, that were not mine: ones I did not share, but which I tried my best to understand.

The Story

In 1985, the massive financial scandals of the late 1980s and early 1990s had not yet exploded in the face of governments, banks, bourses, insurance and industrial concerns. In 1985 therefore, to be told that someone had calmly stolen £40 million was a breathtaking piece of information.

The facts were recounted to me at a meeting in London. Could I recover the money? It was the kind of challenge that appealed to me. If hands were lopped off for the theft of a bicycle, what should be lopped off for a theft of such magnitude?

Many individuals, companies, even rulers, had lost heavily as a result of the insouciance and cunning of the managing director of the development company concerned. He had convinced them all of the importance of the project (Arab countries, though immeasurably wealthy, were also developing countries), of his good faith, status, and experience (which were undeniable), and of the golden prospects ahead for investors. What he did not tell them was that he was afflicted by the universal deadly sin of the decade – greed.

My question to the representative of the company and their lawyer was, 'Why London?' The offence had been committed abroad. Legal judgments had been obtained in the courts abroad. Funds were likely to be abroad, or spread about the many offshore resting places conveniently provided for such purposes. The answer was that the criminal was living in London. If pressure could be brought on him, the threat, or even the actuality, of a period of custody, would impel him to disclose the whereabouts of the assets, even to disgorge them.

I expressed my doubts. A man who had brazenly told a meeting of directors that he had just taken £40 million of the company's money for his own use was unlikely to succumb to a threat of prison. Likewise, a man whose photograph and details had been circulated worldwide by the International Police Organisation (Interpol) under the heading 'Wanted, International Criminal', was unlikely to worry about the kind of action we could take in the English courts.

I studied the Interpol details, 'body – stocky, hair colour – grey, nose – rather big, face – round, shape – ordinary, speech – slow, forehead – wide, walking – slow, attitude – calm'. Calm, indeed. This was no individual to be flustered and frightened by the gradating, terraced processes of the law.

However, despite my doubts, I was urged to take whatever action I could. Something had to be done. A report had to be given to those whose pockets and bank accounts were lighter and much reduced by the nefarious activities of this calm, slow-walking director with the rather large nose. Basic details of his whereabouts and movements were obtained through enquiry agents. My colleagues and I studied the law.

English common law is a great gift to the world. It still influences at least one third of the world's legal systems. Like most things in England, it developed pragmatically, often a by-product of tension between king, barons, Church and Parliament. It developed a jury system, originally based on the personal knowledge of the accused by the jury, a process subsequently completely reversed.

It produced Magna Carta, 'To no man will we deny, to no man delay, justice' – a wonderful ideal not always observed in practice. It created the idea of judicial precedent, a kind of follow-my-leader in decision making, often binding the future, yet providing a sense of certainty to lawyers and litigants. It produced a remedial system of equity to compensate for the stiffness of the common law courts. It gave rise to influential, authoritative legal commentators – Bracton, Coke, Blackstone, Dicey, Denning. It became the bulwark of the liberty of the individual against the dominance of established authority.

One of its significant aspects was the institution of particular writs to meet particular wrongs. If a writ could issue, then a wrong could be put right. Thus developed the law of torts – civil wrongs. As law students, we waded through medieval legal history. We noted that a Statute of Westminster in 1285 gave a boost as to which writ could issue. Much of it was in Latin. I came to realise why, never having seen a Latin word before the age of 16, I had to study furiously this ancient tongue in the succeeding two years in order to pass examinations giving entry to law school. Cicero's *Pro Murena* speech become my bedside reading. I knew it by heart. Virgil's *Georgics* probably stimulated my later interest in husbandry and ecology, as did Livy in themes of historical study.

This early development in new paths in English law was paralleled by a later similar expansion. Since 1945, the whole area of judicial review, whereby judges took into their purview the processes of administration and decision-making, flourished from a small seed into a powerful tree, to the frequent consternation of governmental ministers and departments. Similarly new writs and orders were activated by the courts, which my colleagues and I felt might help in the case of our calm embezzler.

The courts discovered new ways. They could issue an Anton Pillar Order, a Mareva Order, which could really put a defendant's back against the wall. His assets in the country could be frozen where they were. They could not be transferred. He had to swear on oath, a document detailing his assets anywhere in the world in which he had a direct or indirect interest. He had to give documentary proof of everything. He could be prevented from leaving the United Kingdom and his passport taken from him. He could be allowed but a pittance from his assets to live on.

This was powerful ammunition. First we had to register the foreign judgement in our own courts (as we could in this case), serve a writ, and at the same time, convince a judge that it was right to make these enormous inroads into the privacy and liberty of a citizen or resident.

We put these procedures into motion, but I also felt that I had to have a look at our potential adversary. I did. It opened up for me yet another world – the luxurious nocturnal domain of the casinos and the gaming table.

Mayfair and nearby St. James is the most fashionable part of London. It occupies an area between Oxford Street to the north, Piccadilly extending to Pall Mall to the south, Park Lane to the west and Regent Street to the east. It contains some of the most expensive properties in Britain, distinguished 18th century houses, famous clubs and embassies, the capital's foremost classical restaurants, great fashion houses, and some delightful green squares (a planning inheritance from its Georgian forbears). It is an area always in demand. Benjamin Disraeli lived in Park Lane and Curzon Street, Robert Clive (of India) in Berkeley Square. To its south, parade a string of royal palaces; to the north and east, vast retail emporia; to the west, the wide acres and waters of royal Hyde Park. Mayfair has always been a centre for gambling in comfort.

As 1980s money washed around London, entrepreneurs opened elaborate clubs to attract and catch some of it. Prestigious, elegant buildings were converted in Park Lane, Curzon Place, Berkeley Square, across the face of Mayfair.

In search of our slow-speaking, slow-walking quarry, my Arab colleagues and I toured the resplendently decorated clubs, observed their magnificent chandeliers, gilded French furniture, sweeping staircases, rich deep carpets. We entered many gaming-rooms. To me they exuded an air of sadness. Thousands, sometimes tens of thousands, of pounds were launched on a single game, a single number. The participants may have felt a sense of excitement, even power. Smart men in dinner suits and expressionless, svelte women in low-cut dresses distributed the pieces almost automatically after each throw had ended, after each circle of the wheel.

We understood our human objective often had bodyguards accompanying him. We noticed security men in corridors, outside lifts. It seemed a miserable way of enjoying oneself, yet it had become a status symbol, and, as far as their home countries were concerned, a kind of act of defiance.

At about midnight, hunger overtook us. We dined in one of the clubs off magnificently prepared and cooked food, whose quality the *Michelin* and *Good Food Guide* would describe with ecstasy, had they access to the premises. Big gamblers, it seemed, were allowed to eat free. Our hunted man stated later, on oath, that he was allowed to dine 'on the house' as, 'My presence at the clubs tends to attract wealthy gamblers with whom I previously associated'.

Eventually, in the early morn, we found him. Interpol was out of date. They should have amended their description. The shape was far from ordinary. He was corpulent. His face, not merely his hair, was grey, whilst the heavy bags under his eyes could have contained a good proportion of the missing forty million.

My friend shook hands with him, identifying him, just as Judas had kissed Jesus. I did not talk to him. I was taken aback by his aged appearance. I had an opportunity to watch him carefully. He was on his guard; serious, self-contained, stocky certainly; probably aware of being observed. Our object achieved, we left.

We stepped into the cool, fresh air of the street. A parade of chauffeured Rolls-Royces waited patiently in attendance. The gamblers would soon depart. I had had enough of casinos and gambling, and preceded them.

We were dealing, I decided, with a very determined, but somewhat dilapidated, customer. I returned to our law books and writs, enlivened by a glimmer of the world of cushioned, casual wealth. Court procedures followed quickly.

His passport was surrendered. We learned of other countries, other financial houses, on his heels for the same offence. We were fascinated with his collection of Rolls-Royces, Mercedes, and Lagondas, girl friends with fur coats in maintained flats, the vast range of shares, none directly owned by him. Assets were in the names of his wife, children, relatives. I was reminded of the old Cockney who, when told during the wartime bombing blitz that 'If your name's on it, there's nothing you can do', replied 'I'm alright then. Everything's in my wife's name'.

It was discovered that the embezzler's house was one of 20 or more in the district owned by his family. He owned nothing. He had nothing. The £40 million had disappeared on the Stock Exchange, or in misjudged purchases on the futures market. How did he live then? His own words, 'In my country it is a matter of honour, as well as social and cultural tradition, that those with the wealth in any extended family provide for its other members'. Provide gambling chips? Honour?

There were no assets we could touch. We could only touch him. Back we went to court, indicated what we had discovered – that the defendant was not being frank (could that ever be expected?), that he saw justice 'running up behind him from over his shoulder', that the strongest action was necessary. We persuaded the judge to issue, for the fifth time only in 80 years, a writ Ne Exeat Regno – a royal prerogative writ. The collection of Orders we obtained made legal history, a combined assault on this criminal adventurer.

The Ne Exeat Regno writ is unusually worded. It is addressed to the tipstaff of the Supreme Court – an almost Dickensian touch – 'and to all constables and other peace officers whom it may concern'. It mentions the indebtedness, and that the defendant 'designs quickly to go into parts beyond the seas, as by oath in that behalf appears, which tends to the great prejudice and damage of the complainants'. It enjoins the tipstaff to bring the creator of the great injustice to the court, into custody, if he could not provide bail or security in the modest sum of the equivalent of £40 million.

When faced by a phalanx of the awesome tipstaff, his constables, et al., he went quietly into custody. We had achieved what we had been asked to do. His extended family never lifted a finger. No money was forthcoming. We had taken the law to the limit of its jurisdiction. It could go no further.

A day or two later another judge began to talk about the liberty of the subject. We knew then we had reached the end of a road.

Eventually the man's passport was returned, probably one of several he possessed. Soon the gambling clubs became aware they had lost one of their star customers and attractions.

We caught up with him later in North Africa, where again prison walls embraced him. He was shipped back to his country of origin, who had lost so much by his machinations, and they promptly released him. I pondered, other countries, other ways; my ways, your ways; my thoughts, your thoughts; my extended family, your extended family; my honour, your honour.

Within a few years, his accumulated experience weighed even more heavily on him. He could not escape his past, his actions, himself. He deteriorated.

Before he reached the age of 50 he was summoned to another court, another judgment. No writ Ne Exeat Regno, nor any writ, could reach him in the world beyond. He may indeed have been gambling on futures, but had finally come face to face with a future he had not anticipated. What had he achieved by his greed, his ostentation, his scheming? Nothing but an early death, without honour. The Lord's will? Inshallah? Perhaps.

Chapter XVIII

The One-Day Case

Introduction

When William Shakespeare wrote of the law's delay, or Charles Dickens was planning *Bleak House*, they could never have envisaged a case being completed within a mere 24 hours.

That is what happened to me, once. An unusual affair certainly; no courts, no 'm' Luds', no tortuous procedure.

When, in 1952, I commenced legal practice in Fleet Street, a stone's throw from the château-like creation reverently described as the Supreme Court of Justice, alias the Law Courts, there were, I must admit, times when I was sorely tempted to open my window and heave as many stones as I could in its direction, so tried and tested was I by the eerie rules of procedure, enshrined in something we solicitors call the White Book.

That book has expanded into several volumes. It is the major source of exasperation for clients, and the frustration of practitioners, though drawn up by a committee of Lord High This, Master That, et al., to see fair play all along the line between litigating combatants.

The case of David which follows never involved a single faceless form, an ingratiating 'If you please, your Lordship, your Worship, your Majesty', merely a bout of common sense and a little knowledge of what was going on in the great world outside of Chancery Lane.

The Story

The year was 1989, the country the Republic of South Africa. What was a London lawyer doing about that far-away place? It was a land I had never visited, although told repeatedly of its great natural beauty. Somehow things had been going on there which did not appeal to me. Whenever I walked through Trafalgar Square, the most efficient means of locomotion there, I noticed protesters outside the Republic's embassy, night and day, filling the pavement with banners, vigils, fasting, reminders of Steve Biko, Nelson Mandela, apartheid, police brutality.

London is full of protesters for one cause or another. It is often difficult to know, without first-hand experience, which agitators are sublimating or satisfying their own personal problems, which group is financed by which overseas government or party, who has a genuine, and who an imagined, grievance.

Yet somehow I felt in my bones that something was rotten in the state of South Africa. That it was a complicated tribal, minority/majority, coloured/black/white, Third World/First World, historical, Boer/Zulu, mining/hostel, left-wing/right-wing mélange or melée emerged clearly from the press and radio. Television pictures, however selective, added to my unease. Too many people failed to emerge alive from police custody, or, if they did, their appearance, faces especially, had strangely altered.

On one drab Thursday in autumnal London, pondering a pile of files on my desk relating to property transfers, companies, charities, commercial issues, hopes of immigrants and potential citizens, I received a telephone call from a desperate mother. It had been suggested by someone, who knew someone else, who had told her daughter, who had passed a message that I might be able to help. Thus solicitors keep in business, by someone who knows somebody else, who is related to a third party who breathes your name, and gets it right, as otherwise the client could finish up with one of the multitudinous Roses who inhabit the holy register of The Law Society.

The mother's concern was real, urgent, vital, elemental. Her son, of whom she was so proud, had been taken into custody and was held in what she described as the most notorious police station in Johannesburg. The police did not have to give any reason for their action. They had almost arbitrary powers under emergency regulations; no White Book rules to bother them, no habeas corpus. They were a law unto themselves, or so it seemed, answerable only to their superiors and, ultimately, the Government.

The mother was desperate. She was passionate but also, in the circumstances, surprisingly fluent, reasoned, and articulate. She had almost come to the end of her tether.

I asked her what terrible crime or misdemeanour her son had committed, or had been about to commit. He was, it appeared, a normal medical student at a noted university, had done nothing in his career remotely connected with criminality or subversion, yet here he was incarcerated for weeks on end, and for what? For teaching English to black students and youngsters.

'For that his liberty was taken from him?', I queried.

'For less than that, people have been taken into custody', I was told.

This was my first contact with a specific case in South Africa. I had been involved in civil rights issues in Britain, and had fought cases through the courts. Two years after David's case, I was involved, though not as a lawyer, in a similar problem. The Nigerian authorities, acting under similar emergency regulations, arbitrarily took into custody a brave man, Dr Biko Ransome-Kuti, a leading proponent of human rights in his country. An international outcry then resulted in his release. Both black and white persecute, both black and white suffer. It is man's inhumanity to man that is the sad, continuous theme.

These experiences had impelled me into responding, in 1989, to the creation of the Commonwealth Human Rights Initiative of which I became treasurer. Anyone less likely to be a treasurer could not be imagined, as my former partners, accountants, financial advisers, could confirm. I had never, throughout my life, known precisely what I possessed, earned, or owed. All I know is that, with the help of the aforesaid professionals and the good Lord above, I remained solvent, kept a roof over my head, and knew where my next meal was coming from. But I was punctilious to the last penny for the Initiative, as for clients.

From my subsequent valuable and enjoyable experience with the Initiative, I learned of the successes and failures in the human rights record of the 53 nations of the Commonwealth: an uneven, varying story, conditioned by history, depressed by bigotry and the lust for power, stimulated by example and fearless courage.

Yet here was South Africa, banished from the Commonwealth family many years before. Here was a young man imprisoned in that country. I asked the mother what she wanted me to do. To get him released, was the reply. Almost to save his future, his life, she implied. She feared the effect solitary incarceration could have on her son in later life.

What had she done? I asked her. She recounted a campaign that would have done justice to a long-established organisation, not merely to a housewife and mother. Her efforts had been remarkable, intense, but unsuccessful.

A lawyer had been appointed in Johannesburg, had visited David, and was trying her best to penetrate the official obscuranticism that rose up forbiddingly, like a wall. Other bodies in the Republic had protested. International support had been recruited, presidents and prime ministers across Europe had been petitioned to help. Religious leaders appealed for intervention. Even the United States Congress had been involved. Yet to no avail.

Living at the time in Yorkshire, she had appeared locally on both radio and television. Newspaper articles set out the plight of the son. She appealed to the Wilberforce Council, a human rights body in Hull, home of the great opponent of slavery. However, nothing, it appeared, could influence the inflexible attitude of the South African authorities. They would not listen.

I could not comprehend why they should worry about a young, innocent student, teaching English. Were they trying to make an example of David? To warn others not to associate, white with black, teacher with pupil?

I thought how I would feel if this had happened to my own children, or children of those close to me.

I saw David's sister immediately, read the papers she had amassed, spoke to the mother, and to others supporting her in her fight. Clearly there was nothing I could do through the English courts. The White Book would remain on its shelf. I could do nothing in the South African legal process. All that could be done was being done. Suddenly I hit on an idea, although not an original one I confess.

I recalled how a Polish-born lawyer, practising in Britain, had successfully appealed by phone to Winston Churchill, then Prime Minister, as a result of which some Poles who had escaped from communist Poland, yet who had been denied admission by H.M. Immigration, were eventually allowed to set foot in Britain. Why then could I not recruit the highest political influence to help? The Prime Minister at the time was Margaret, later Lady, Thatcher. She was single-minded, determined, like her Churchillian predecessor, as controversial as he was, but as concerned as the great war leader with the issues of liberty and human rights.

And the timing for an attempted intervention through Downing Street was exactly right.

Every two years heads of Commonwealth governments assemble to discuss common matters. The mnemonic is CHOGM, Commonwealth Heads of Government Meeting. In 1987, Mrs Thatcher had prevented, at such a meeting, the imposition of full sanctions on South Africa. But the issue was alive, urgent, and within a day or two of that autumnal Thursday, Mrs Thatcher was again off to CHOGM. She was South Africa's only hope, only defence, against a massive escalation of sanctions. She was crucial to the survival of the existing regime in Pretoria. The last thing the South African Government wanted was any development that might inhibit her opposition to the united views of the rest of the Commonwealth leaders.

I therefore proposed to the mother that we place David's plight before the Prime Minister without delay. She agreed instantly. I drew up and agreed with her a form of letter to Mrs Thatcher, informing her of this breach of fundamental human rights by the authorities in Johannesburg, and how the young man was detained in a prison cell for no reason, without any charge being brought against him.

The next morning, Friday, having made arrangements the prior evening with her legal constituency office (she was MP for the area in which we had an office), I entered the elegant portals of 10 Downing Street with my missive. At the same time, the contents of my letter were made known, through the mother and her family, to the South African Ambassador in London. If the latter glanced out of his window he could see the perennial demonstrators down below. On his desk he could read the terms of an accusation lodged with Mrs Thatcher, accusing his lords and masters at home of miserable behaviour to one innocent young man. The Ambassador reacted.

The information was clearly despatched by him at once to his home Government, who were concerned that nothing, however small, should be allowed to insinuate a doubt in the Prime Minister's mind and determination.

By 2.00 p.m. that afternoon David walked out of prison, free – out of jail, and, as the Old Testament puts it, out of the house of bondage. It was a risk, a chance, a long shot, but it paid off. There was great joy among David's family, and Margaret Thatcher, through her personal secretary, responded in the unambiguous terms I had anticipated.

The young man went on to qualify as a doctor and to pursue his good works. He came to London to thank me. In my enthusiasm, I had never mentioned the words money, costs, fees. I told the mother to forget about paying anything. I called it David's day. I was as thrilled for him as if he were my own son.

The mother however promised to take me and my wife for a meal at a leading restaurant. I am still waiting, but does it matter? Man does not live by bread alone ...

Chapter XIX

They Came to a City
or *The New Londoners*

Introduction

I n Cheapside, in the City of London, rises the elegant church of St.
Mary atte Bow. Whoever is born within the sound of its bells, is
regarded as a genuine Londoner, a Cockney to be precise. I was born
within the sound of those bells, and have spent all my life in this
great metropolis.

As a child, I lived on the streets of east London, much as Jewish
youngsters lived on the pavements of New York's East Side. My seaside
was a strip of sand that edged the River Thames at the foot of the
Tower of London. My sports fields were the tarmacked streets or the
gravel pitch in Dickensian Shadwell. Wapping Steps were close by, as
were the once-thriving docks. I fell asleep at night to the blare of
ships' sirens.

I recall those dour men, peaked caps on heads, who, in the 1930s,
marched to London from Jarrow in northern England, protesting
against the humiliation of unemployment; perhaps the best-behaved
protesters ever. Their march ended close to my home, where many
lodged in a local school.

I recall another march, also in the mid-1930s: that of arrogant
black-shirted Mosleyite fascists parading through the streets of
Whitechapel; an act of enormous provocation, successfully opposed
by ordinary decent Londoners. I watched, fascinated, from the
inside of a shop window whose plate glass had been wholly destroyed.

A far more prolonged and severe form of turbulence, a few years
later, was the bombing of London during the Second World War,
when for a time I shared with hundreds of others the nightly
communal bed of an Underground station platform – a scene
strikingly captured by the sketches of Henry Moore.

Anyone who lived in battered London in those uncertain days

cannot but acknowledge the unpayable debt owed to Winston Churchill for his rare courage and leadership. No one who lived through those war years could ever join the intellectual, but uncomprehending, band of historians who try to cast doubt on the unique quality of the great man. But for him, they would have had no opportunity, many years later, to air their views in freedom. There would have been no freedom, and but one history book.

Who can forget the joy of dancing wildly in London's West End in 1945 when the war ended, or the street parties celebrating royal events, coronations, silver jubilees! London has a particularly attractive, quietly welcoming quality, not only for those born there, but for so many who have made it their home. I have encountered a varied host of adopted Londoners who, for whatever reason, came to the city from the furthest corners of the globe, and who sought to set down roots in this once-imperial capital.

Immigrants came en masse from the coloured Commonwealth – India, Pakistan, Bangladesh, Sri Lanka, the West Indies, Africa. A steady stream migrated from the nearby Republic of Ireland, making up the largest ethnic minority in the country. Groups gravitated to specific areas, the Caribbeans to Brixton, the Irish to Kilburn, Poles to west London, Australians to Earls Court.

I recall the characters who sought my help. Many who came wanted the legal right to remain. Many sought advice as to businesses and professions. Others were anxious to bring to London relatives still abroad, and thus unite their families. It is not easy to be an immigrant, to uproot oneself, and adapt to a new world. I remember so many of those from abroad who came to settle in a strange land.

There was the German countess who had hidden Jews in her home in her native Germany throughout the war, and who, aghast at the racism of her people, had come to London after 1945 to work as a domestic servant – the only way she could obtain entry. She remained close to our family till her death 40 years later.

There was the dashing Pole who had escaped from a Colditz-type German prisoner-of-war camp, and whose exploits were later publicly recorded. He settled in London and became an insurance broker, a prosaic life after such earlier excitement.

Another Pole and I became great friends. I had helped his Hungarian countess wife in her claim for compensation for the loss of her Budapest home. Her husband, Major de Hinterhoff, who had been cruelly treated by the Gestapo, had become a military strategist of note. His book *Disengagement,* on ending the East-West confrontation in Europe, became a standard and influential work. He set up the Military Commentators Circle. Monthly I accompanied him to the RAF Club in Piccadilly, where the leading military strategists of the land privately conveyed to assembled military attachés of diplomatic missions their views on issues of the day.

One speaker, explaining his country's defence problems, impressed me with his military knowledge and concern for his country's security. Shimon Peres later became Israel's Prime Minister. In this Circle I listened to British Army Brigadiers, with confident, cultured voices, fighting again, with the aid of wall maps, battles of the recent world war, and of conflicts then erupting from Vietnam to the Sinai Desert. I met Captain Liddell Hart, world-famous military strategist, but was more impressed by his canary-coloured waistcoat than his strategic conceptions.

During one of the Israeli-Egyptian confrontations, a frequent visitor to my office was a famous Egyptian musician. He often brought his lute, and we sat together as he played popular tunes of his country. I learned that relations between individuals could transcend the crude enmity of nationalisms.

Other musicians from abroad also played in my office, not for entertainment, but to illustrate the origin of calypso music. There was a legal dispute. We had to decide whether the famous song 'Mary Ann' was an original composition or a traditional melody. We analysed its rhythms, compared it to well-known calypsoes. Other tenants of the building must have wondered what kind of an office I was running. Much money rested on our decision. The case eventually moved across the Atlantic where, to my amazement, the lawyers involved claimed, as their fee, one third of the total money recovered. I was clearly practising in the wrong country.

At one point I was simultaneously helping two people from Jerusalem to obtain a right of settlement, one an Arab, the other a Jew. The Arab was ostracised, threatened, by his fellow-Muslims because he had married a Christian. The Jew, a computer scientist, sought to set up a business in London. Nationalities, creeds, races, were at nought when there was a purpose to be achieved, advice to be given.

Then there was the caring Trinidad businesswoman who told her daughter she would try and help her with her studies. The daughter decided this represented a binding legal agreement on the mother to finance her student efforts for years and years. She took the helpful, but deeply hurt, mother as far as the Court of Appeal, which rightly dismissed the case. It has since become a leading case on the law of intention to create legal relations.

Many people tried to settle and work in London. A new strand developed in my work, that of immigration law. I was asked to help people of every background – Arabs, Jews, Armenians, Chinese, South Americans, Spaniards – all intent on having the right to live and work in the metropolis. London became a world and a city. I enlarged my education. I learned about the history, geography, religions, and customs of distant lands and their peoples. Being a lawyer was not merely learning and applying the law but, for me, an ongoing process of education in the anatomy and function of human society and its individual components. The immigrants were my teachers. I am indebted to them.

Among the saddest problems caused by the Cold War was the separation of families by the Iron Curtain that divided Europe from 1945 until the crumbling of the Berlin Wall and the communist regimes in 1989. Of those from Eastern Europe who reached Britain, the majority claimed political asylum. But first they had to prove to the satisfaction of the Home Office, and, if not accepted, then to a tribunal, that they had a real and well-founded fear of persecution should they be returned to their native land.

Frequently it was difficult to prove this ever-present fear of persecution. Evidence was hard to obtain. Not all applicants were genuine, but in each case I had to study the nature of the particular totalitarian regime, whether Iraq, the Soviet Union, or a war-rent African state, and the danger to life and limb for the particular claimant if returned there. What follows is an illustration of this problem.

The Story

During the 50 years that followed the Second World War, Britain's population rose by a third, from forty-two million to fifty-six million, partly, but not primarily, due to immigration. As a result, immigration and nationality laws were gradually tightened. It became harder to enter Britain and settle permanently. Some politicians saw a relationship between the two sets of laws, just as others view a strict control of immigration as the basis of good race relations. There may or may not be truth in such views, but many who came from the Commonwealth found this approach ironical in view of long British control of, and settlement in, their home countries.

Nationality laws from 1948 to 1981, and immigration legislation from 1962 to 1988, increasingly restricted rights of entry and settlement. Refugees and those claiming political asylum found it harder to satisfy the authorities. The power of immigration officers at sea ports and air ports increased correspondingly.

How often did I receive a call, not always at the most acceptable hour of the day or night, to hasten to London's Heathrow Airport, where a new arrival was about to be shipped back whence he or she had come, or else placed in a detention centre. Yet immigration officers had a hard task, as so many who came to this land merely pretended to be visitors, but once allowed in, remained and disappeared into the community.

The honest often suffered through the machinations of the deceitful. There were a range of people, usually from the West Indies, well settled in Britain, who never left or returned to the country without my professional card in their pocket, since so often they expected, and received, a hostile and suspicious reception when they re-entered the country.

As many countries fell under the sway of dictatorship or mass brutality, many who escaped sought asylum in Britain. Lebanon in the 1980s was a murderous place. One hundred thousand people perished in a barbaric civil war. Among them was a businessman, cruelly murdered, his body not found for 11 days. His widow frantically escaped from the country, fearful for her life. She rang me from an island in the Mediterranean.

The Home Office in London was understanding. It often is, if approached frankly. It allowed her to enter Britain as a refugee. She was eternally grateful. Both she and Britain gained from that decision. She is one of the sweetest-natured persons I have met, and she and her family have remained good friends. Sharing the ordeal of a refugee sometimes creates a common bond of sympathy and understanding between lawyer and client.

Britain has a proud record in taking in people fleeing from political or religious prosecution. She opened her gates to the

Huguenots in the 16th century, to Italian refugees in the mid-19th century, to Jews from Eastern Europe and Nazi Germany during the present century. Those who came exchanged fear for freedom, whilst Britain gained from the enterprise and ability of the new residents.

As the last decade of this century moves on, Britain is again wrestling with the problem, trying to reconcile her tradition of welcoming refugees with the prospect of an unparalleled number seeking entry. At the same time, she is trying to conform with United Nations and European Conventions and Declarations on human rights and the status of refugees. It is an unenviable dilemma, leading sometimes to hasty, ill-thought-out legislation.

During the 1970s and 1980s, however, much effort was directed, by individuals and organisations to assisting those fleeing from the heartless misery of communism. The battles of the 'refusniks' – the dissidents – helped to raise the banner of human rights in countries where such rights existed only in their hypocritical constitutions.

Czechoslovakia was one such country that suffered from the iron grip of Marxist dogmatism. Now that the Iron Curtain has vanished, it is easy to forget the ghastliness of communist regimes. The liberal Czechoslovakia of Benes and Masaryk had been displaced by a doctrinaire regime that wiped the smiles from the faces of all her citizens.

A glowing constitution had been proclaimed by the regime in 1967. It boasted, 'Exploitation of man by man has been eliminated forever. The entire cultural policy shall be directed in the spirit of the scientific world outlook – Marxism-Leninism'. In a burst of enthusiasm it guaranteed 'the free and complete expression of the personality of the individual', as well as 'the equality of all citizens without regard to nationality and race'. 'The society of working people shall ensure equal opportunities in all fields of public life', including the right to education and work, whilst 'freedom of expression in all field of public life, freedom of speech, of the press' were guaranteed, as well as 'freedom of assembly, to hold public parades and demonstrations'.

Above all 'The inviolability of the person, the home, the privacy of mails, shall be guaranteed', in addition to 'the right to profess any religious faith, and to practise religious beliefs in so far as this does not contravene the law'.

It sounded like a recipe for paradise. Yet so many people were eager to escape. The constitution was, of course, a typical communist sham, a fraud. The Czechs and Slovaks suffered patiently in this repressive police state. When I asked the intellectual young man who sought my help why he wished to remain in Britain, he replied, 'We just want to live a decent, free, unoppressed, uncensored life'.

He had been allowed out of the Prague paradise in the hope that his visit to London, and his artistic efforts, would produce hard currency for the regime. Half of any money he earned abroad had to be surrendered to the state. Whilst away, he had been asked to spy on his colleagues – nothing unusual for such a regime.

A 1973 law had made it a crime to leave the country without permission; a law in breach of every recognised convention on human rights. Those who had done so, and had innocently returned under a special amnesty, found to their cost that socialist legality extended to abuse, threats and beatings, as well as cynical dishonouring of rights enshrined in the law.

Furthermore, going abroad with permission and failing to return on the due date was also a serious crime, punishable with a prison sentence, apart from other disabilities when finally released.

As a famous Czech-born dramatist wrote, in support of the young man's appeal for political asylum in Britain:

'The very desire to live abroad can be enough to make a Czechoslovak citizen *persona non grata* with all the consequent persecutions'.

The Times described the state of affairs as 'The new barbarism'. A young Czech who was interested in American beat and rock music, and who had invited some friends home to hear his musical tapes, received a 15-year prison sentence for espionage. Indeed a new barbarism or dark ages.

The State was paramount. Anyone could be labelled a traitor. Its tentacles reached into every aspect of family life. Even a child's name had to be taken from a permitted list of names.

But the young Czech discussing his affairs with me had two further problems with his home country: as a Jew, he faced a special and insidious form of racism, and as the son of a well-known father who had also not long before left the country and failed to return, he faced larger problems. Czech authorities had a way of visiting the 'sins' of parents on their children, and on their children's children.

If my client returned from London, he would be treated as a hostage, a scapegoat; he would be unable to find suitable employment, when joblessness was a crime under the Catch-22 constitution; his children would be ineligible for higher education; and after serving a prison sentence for his late return, he would never again be allowed to leave the country.

Once in London, he told me, he had applied for asylum. His application concentrated on religious or ethnic persecution as a Jew, rather than on the extent of political and personal danger. He had the standard interview with the Home Office.

He was unprepared. He never explained to the interviewer the extent of his fear: he had twice been stripped naked at the border; the police were constantly harassing him, calling at his home; his brother had been prevented from leaving the country; he was obliged to participate in political meetings, parades and indoctrination courses. Since his father, whose name was widely-known, had repudiated the country by not returning, he, the son, with the same surname, would become a marked man, open to denunciations, false charges, fabricated evidence – constant features of Marxist morality.

None of this did he mention at the interview. When I asked him why he had made no mention of these matters, he replied that he assumed the British authorities were fully aware of what went on in communist countries. But the interviewing officer naturally reported only on what he had been told. Hence the application was refused. Thus he came to me to help with his appeal.

Fortunately there was time to appeal and a legal aid system to help, albeit modestly, with the costs of the appeal. In such cases, where a person's liberty, possibly his life, was at stake, I was rarely concerned with the issue of legal costs, to the despairing and justified consternation of my colleagues.

We ranged far and wide to amass detailed evidence which would substantiate our client's legitimate fears. We found much support from Members of Parliament, writers, organisations, case reports, individuals who had themselves escaped. All this we collated and presented to the Home Office, who still were not satisfied and insisted on a full hearing before an immigration appeal tribunal.

The onus was on us. The young man gave evidence. I questioned him in detail. He told how his father, who was celebrated in the country, became, after the Soviet invasion of 1968 and the uprooting of the smallest shoots of freedom, a non-person, whose name was not allowed to be mentioned in public. The father had survived a concentration camp. It made no difference.

All the father's international activities were stopped, public appearances banned, his whole existence drastically changed. The son would now suffer the same fate, and more. He would bear the brunt of the hatred and the frustration of the authorities at not being able to reach his escaped father. He explained that to return to Prague, once his father had left the country, was not possible. Life would be hell for him, his wife and children.

The questioning and the cross-questioning of the client and his witnesses continued throughout the day. The case was not concluded, but the evidence had impressed the Home Office representative. He asked to adjourn the hearing so that the facts could again be reviewed. We never went back to the tribunal.

Shortly afterwards a letter arrived. The Home Office had looked again at the evidence, especially the new and independent evidence. The Secretary of State had changed his mind (it does happen), reversed his former decision, and decided to grant the family political asylum. Great was the joy, the rejoicing, the gratitude. The future of a family had been saved. They were grateful to Britain for taking them in and allowing them to remain. The dark cloud of fear had been lifted from them.

This is but a brief record of a single case – one that succeeded. Many did not, sometimes because they were not genuine, sometimes because of deficient language interpreters, sometimes because applicants assumed British authorities knew about conditions in their home country and that no further elaboration was required, sometimes because advice organisations treated the cases routinely, whereas each case involved the happiness and liberty of more than one individual, one family.

Thus the client, his wife, and their children, took their place in society as part of the expanding world of new Londoners. Gradually they adjusted, adapted, and settled into the ways of a free and open society. In time they would become just plain Londoners, hopefully never forgetting the nature of life under a totalitarian heel, but, hopefully too, never taking for granted the great privilege of liberty that rang out from the bells of London to all her citizens.

Chapter XX

Law of the Land

or *Farewell Leicester Square*

Introduction

T he Psalmist may have proclaimed, 'The Earth is the Lord's and the fulness thereof', but monarchs and parliaments had other ideas. The old Mosaic law had simple rules about land. It could not be worked every seventh day, had to rest every seventh year, was not to be held in single ownership longer than seven times seven years. These rules somehow tried to show respect for the land, as well as our impermanence as mere sojourners here. Human beings arrived, lived a span of three score years and ten (in some cases a little more), then departed, but the land and the Lord remained forever.

Throughout history, armies have fought over ownership and possession of land. They still do. It represents wealth, food, water, security. In 1066, when William of Normandy took control of England, he parcelled out the country among his chieftains, who subdivided smaller pieces to others in return for payment or services. The theory still holds that all land ultimately belongs to the monarch, as equally all justice and honour emanate from that same source.

The prospective lawyer, however, has to contend with the difficult study of the law of real property, freehold property; the evolution over a thousand years of patterns of ownership and rights in, over, and under, land. When first confronted with a textbook on the subject, it made as much sense to me as a work in a language I did not know, on a subject I could not comprehend.

I learned about frankalmoign, knight service, gavelkind, copyhold, socage tenure, uses, entails. But gradually light began to dawn. Later, being an athletic type, I was happier with the notion of 'covenants running with the land'. Electricity experts would take easily to the concept of positive and negative covenants.

An enormous body of law built up before 1925, in which year, the *annus mirabilis* of modern real property, everything changed. The law of land emerged from the manorial class system into the age of burgeoning equality.

Yet law students, poor creatures, had to learn not only the new, but also the old: the novel expanding pattern of registration of title and ownership in a state-operated Land Registry, but also the long-evolved, wordy, unregistered conveyancing system, familiar to laymen in endless pages of exquisite calligraphy adorning sturdy parchment sheets, much in demand as lampshades, or framed as pictures on the wall.

Just as this revolutionary 20th century has witnessed radical change in ownership law, so too a flood of laws emerged as to what a person could, or could not do, with his land. It used to be asserted that an Englishman's home was his castle. He could go ahead and indeed build a castle on it, whether of brick, wood, stone or sand, without seeking a nod of consent from anyone.

But all has now changed. Planning laws have sprouted and flourished, embracing every sod of earth, every blade of grass in the kingdom. You may own your land, your home, your business, but you cannot do what you like with it. The voice of the planner is heard everywhere; a voice – give it its due – empowered to regulate and modify uninhibited personal ambitions for the social benefit and protection of the community.

Town and country planning, like religion, recognises that no man is an island; that while there are more and more of us walking the face of this particular island, there is no corresponding expansion of land surface; and that therefore we have to make the best use of the land, inflicting as little harm on our neighbour as possible.

It is an admirable social concept, enshrined in a torrent of Town and Country Planning Acts, Regulations, Orders, guidance circulars, and, more recently, European Community Directives, that have flooded lawyers' offices over the last half-century. As the economy blossomed, so development of land expanded. To meet the demand for advice on laws whose terminology occasionally passed all understanding, planning departments multiplied in the larger law firms; multiplied and flourished, at least as long as the boom years of the 1980s lasted.

I was not immune from the planning explosion. My daughter

became a town planner. I read her master's thesis on urban planning with admiration (typical father). I was frequently consulted by individuals, amenity societies, companies; especially where injustice and authority seemed to prevail over common sense and public good. The richer the person or authority, the less respect was shown for the planning process, the more pressure exerted on planning decisions.

I recall an amenity society, representing 800 local citizens, up in arms at the contempt shown to the local planning authority by a wealthy businessman. Strict conditions as to area of building and number of floors were laid down by the council. These were ignored.

The authority was urged to use enforcement procedure to prevent further abuse. Eventually they did. The owner appealed. The Secretary of State appointed an inspector to hold a local inquiry. The appeal, in the idiotic way the law sometimes works, was 'deemed' to operate as a further application for planning permission – an unjust procedure if ever there was one. Planning law has a lot of 'deeming'.

For days I did battle on behalf of the local citizenry against leading Queen's Counsel. I was incensed at the arrogance of wealth, and its blatant disregard for the law. But the law itself was weak and flabby, when it should have been firm and clear, and the issue died out in a compromise decision.

Fighting planning appeals are expensive operations. I have wondered whether there should not be some planning 'friend of the community', just as in children's cases there is often a 'next friend'. There may be free advice centres, but something more is required.

In a delightfully sylvan, quiet London suburb, a developer decided to build a house in the middle of his rear garden: a substantial house, overlooking all adjacent neighbours. The latter, appalled at the invasion of their privacy, joined together. Again we fought the battle of amenity against money, civilised conservation against mercenary aggrandisement. It is often an unequal battle. The stakes are high. The local planning authority hesitated but, fortified by private and public pressure, stiffened their sinews and joined us.

Three separate government-nominated inspectors reported on three separate occasions. There was determination on both sides. Eventually we won this planning football match by two reports to one, a victory that safeguarded the future happiness not only of our clients, but of every household in the street. Back-garden development was halted.

Land is an emotive issue. Every lawyer can tell of the murderous instincts aroused in householders whose neighbours may have encroached an inch, even a centimetre, over the boundary line. Ownership of land echoes deeply in the soul of most people. Development of land strikes just as deeply. Superficially, the issues are clear – the need for planning permissions, prevention of green-belt intrusions, guarding conservation areas – but deep-down there lies the concern, often unconscious, of assaults on personal security, on a way of life, on one's future itself. Good planning, after consultation, can be a boon: bad planning a disaster.

Few bodies of law are quite so technical, so weighed down by jargon, verbiage, and procedure as the planning law, yet it conceals matters of fundamental moment for the well-being of society. Not only is the small householder, or the major property company affected, but, on occasions, world-famous metropolitan centres. It even became a *casus belli* in celebrated Leicester Square, deep in the throbbing heart of London.

The Story

When, in the First World War, soldiers went off to fight in Flanders fields, the song 'It's a long way to Tipperary' was often on their lips, containing the evocative words, 'Goodbye Piccadilly, farewell Leicester Square'.

Thus the troops paid tribute to two centres of London that glowed with love and life, theatre and music; areas that contrasted strikingly with the mud, gloom and death that lay ahead of the departing men. They acknowledged these two spots as the essence of London, referred to sometimes as the 'hub of the Empire', if not of the world. A slight exaggeration, yet these were parts of London held in warm affection.

In the previous century, Leicester Square had been privately owned, much of it by the Tulk family. In the mid-19th century, one of the Tulks sold the central part of the Square to one Elms, on condition that Elms could not build on it. Elms agreed; covenanted accordingly. It then passed into the ownership of one Moxhay, who knew all about the covenant, ignored it, and began construction. What a profitable site for a developer, he must have thought.

Tulk and his clan, who had retained adjacent land, were alarmed by Moxhay's efforts. Building in the Square would affect the value of land they had retained. That was the point of the restriction. Elms had paid but a small sum originally because of the restrictive or negative covenant which affected him, the land, and any buyer who looked at the title deeds. Tulk was upset, marched along to court, and won the day. The covenant bound enterprising builder Moxhay. No building was permitted.

This saga of the relationship between Mr Tulk and Mr Moxhay is engrained on the hearts and minds of every law student in the common law world, prominent in every textbook on the law of the land.

Little did I think, just as 1988 was saying farewell, that I would become involved with that same case affecting that same piece of land. Yet so it happened.

Twenty-five years after the encounter between Tulk and Moxhay, there arose a public-spirited Member of Parliament, one Albert Grant, who gathered to himself all the separately-owned pieces of the Square, 14 in all, and generously donated them to the public.

Ownership of the Square became vested in a body known as the Metropolitan Board of Works, whence it wound its way from public owner to public owner until finally, in 1971, it came to rest, and vest, in the secure arms of the City Council of Westminster.

Albert had expressed the wish that the land be 'preserved for ever for the free use and enjoyment of the public'. Should one venture into the Square today, whether through the Isaac Newton, William Hogarth, Joshua Reynolds, or William Hunter Gates, past the delightfully expressive statue of Charlie Chaplin, those self-same words can be observed boldly engraved on a plinth supporting the stone figure of the immortal William Shakespeare in pensive mood. The activities of Tulk, Moxhay, Grant and Council, I am sure, never crossed that fertile mind.

Yet Mr Albert Grant's brain was much engrossed in a covenant that had enjoined him, and which he had passed on, to convert the ground into 'an ornamental garden or pleasure ground', the only thing permitted in, on, or under, the land being statues, supporting pedestals, seats, and fountains. Nothing could be clearer, and so the position remained from 1874 until 1988.

It was the 'under' that brought clients to my office (or rather me to the clients), namely an association of local citizens concerned at proposals to undermine the status quo. Westminster Council, in their wisdom, had given the London Electricity Board planning permission to place a substation under the Square. They had given the electricity board a 999 year lease of the 'under' area, in return for which they received a substantial sum, which they believed would help appreciably their plans to smarten the appearance of the Square, particularly by extensive pedestrianisation.

It was no small building that was to be placed underground, but a vast construction (Moxhay must have looked down with envy and admiration) measuring 43 metres by 18 metres, and 12 metres deep. The prospect for adjacent businesses, cinemas, banks, seemed bleak. A huge hole was to be created and 15,000 cubic metres of earth removed, requiring the to-ing and fro-ing of scores of lorries, daily, for 80 weeks. Everyone with a business in or close to the Square had a genuine apprehension at the effect this major operation would have on their trade and amenities.

There were other fears. Would foundations of nearby buildings be affected? Was there a fire or security risk? Would there be sufficient ventilation down below to restrict deleterious fumes spreading above the surface? Was subsidence in adjacent buildings a possibility? Would the trees and lawns, such a pleasant feature in an urban environment, be truncated? Above all, in difficult trading times, would visitors be deterred from coming to the Square by the noise and dust that works on this scale would undoubtedly involve? Leicester Square was part of the Soho Conservation Area, a designation recognising its communal importance and severely restricting development of any kind.

I met representatives of the association, which had been formed to safeguard the rights and welfare of those involved in local businesses or who worked locally. We discussed their fears, their prolonged negotiations with the Council and the London Electricity Board. The latter indicated they had studied every alternative, but had a statutory duty to meet rising electricity demand and no satisfactory alternative had presented itself, other than siting a substation of this bulk in the bowels of Leicester Square.

The association, in its methodical way, had obtained a report from a tree expert, indicating inevitable loss of some trees and likely effect on others. Nothing could be done about the planning permission already granted by the self-same Council for the siting of thesub-station in the Square . We had to consider whether the law could help in other ways.

Acts of Parliament were studied, procedures discussed. The only possibility seemed to be judicial review procedure, to see whether Westminster had acted fairly. We thought of a few questions. Did the Council act beyond its jurisdiction? Was it in breach of procedure, of natural justice? Did it act properly as an administrative body in a way that adversely affected a public right? Was there an error in law? Was the Council's decision so absurd that no reasonable council could have taken it? Experts thought it was worth a try, even though it was a slim chance. However, public ventilation of the issue might result in second thoughts about the scheme.

Westminster responded. In their view, they had followed all procedures correctly, had considered all alternatives, had consulted the public, had breached no law, had balanced the inevitable disruption – necessary though regrettable – against the long-term interests of citizens. It sounded reasonable on both sides.

During the investigation, I had read the book *London Under London* by Hillman and Trench (John Murray), which took the reader on a journey, not as deep as Jules Verne's, but at least sufficiently below London's surface to consider what had been going on beneath the Square and district for generations. There is a whole world down below: pipes, wires, sewers, the Underground. There was even the remnants of an old river. To all this was now to be added this electricity-creating rectangle of metal. No wonder the association was worried.

Meanwhile, thoughts turned to the munificent Albert Grant and his covenant. No one was supposed to put anything under the Square. The association, aware of the uncertain outcome of any court case, nevertheless took their courage in their hands and decided on a long shot. So we went to court. Albert and his covenant were thought to be at the heart of the matter. After all, the covenant specifically said that nothing but statues, seats, and fountains within neat iron railings were to be built on the land, and nothing, but nothing, under the land.

Yet, as it transpired, the case turned not on Albert but on a narrow legal point. We contended that the Council and the Electricity Board could not ignore the covenant; that everything they had done –

planning permission, lease – every procedure they had adopted, contravened the letter and the spirit of the law as contained in the covenant. To a layman that would have seemed elementary common sense.

The court, in the person of Mr Justice Simon Brown, sat, listened, deliberated, then pronounced judgement in crystal-clear English, a model for lawyers and educationalists, maintaining the tradition of clarity of expression established by the inimitable Alfred, Lord Denning.

The judge ranged over past statutes and decided cases, as is the wont of judges. He looked at the Open Spaces Act, 1906, which directed local authorities who acquired land for the purpose of open space to keep it as open space – a fairly obvious conclusion. He delved into the legislation, came up with the Local Government Act, 1972, which stated that a council could 'dispose of land held by them in any manner they wish' – not so good. But he also found other words in the Act which restricted local authorities from disposing of land in breach of any trust, covenant or agreement. Progress?

He did not forget Albert and his covenant. He asked himself three questions. The first concerned the mobility of the covenant: Did it run with the land? He found that it did, and was still capable of movement even after 115 years of perpetual motion. The covenant never went to sleep, even if Albert did. In support, he quoted the advice of Westminster's very own leading counsel that there was no doubt that 'The construction of the substation would be a breach of the 'under' covenant, if that covenant is still enforceable'.

The second question the judge asked was whether the benefit of the covenant ran for the benefit of adjoining land – a crucial element in the running process. He looked at the wording, the facts, and replied in the affirmative. We were encouraged. It looked like progress.

He posed a third query. Had anything happened since 1874 to render the covenant inoperative? Westminster's lawyers asserted that a long time had passed, that there were ways now of discharging or modifying old covenants which might once have been relevant but had ceased to be so in this modern age.

There was some truth in this. Conveyancers constantly came up against old covenants, ostensibly still in force, yet more honoured in the breach than in the observance. How often old covenants restrict a house to one occupation when, for years, it had been in multi-occupation. Obviously a breach, but no one worried. So often no one could be found with a right to enforce, or release, these old covenants. No one really wished to go through a Land's Tribunal procedure to nullify them. The common practice, therefore, was to persuade an insurance company to indemnify a buyer against any claim made under them.

It was different in our case. We had a living covenant, running with the Square, able to flex its muscles and impose itself. The judge opined that the covenant was annexed to the land and passed to each successive owner, even if its existence was unknown to he who had acquired the land, the latter thereby possessing 'a hidden treasure which may be discovered in the hour of need'. If the learned judge decided the covenant was in force, how did this affect the case?

If Albert's covenant applied, then it would not be unreasonable for a layman to conclude that both Council and Electricity Board were acting in breach of it. Between them, they, their engineers and planners, were diving underground, then surfacing, leaving their substation behind them, ignoring completely the wishes of the late Mr Grant.

But laymen should never jump to obvious conclusions. The 1972 Act told Councils not to dispose of land where there was a covenant preventing disposal. Albert's covenant never prevented the Council from selling their interest in any part of the Square. All Albert had done was to reach beyond his mortal remains to enjoin whoever owned the land to keep it as an open space for public enjoyment. We were reaching the point lawyers enjoy, getting camels through eyes of needles. Albert was concerned with how the Square was used, not with who owned it.

The association's counsel pointed out that the whole purpose of the council's actions involved a breach of the long-running covenant. The lessee was being obliged to breach the covenant, and Westminster was party to it. It sounded convincing, common sense. The judge called counsel's argument persuasive, but he didn't agree. Judges have to administer the law, not common sense.

Even if the planned project was in breach of the covenant, he ruled, the lease granted by Westminster to the Electricity Board was a separate and distinct step. The disposal, by itself, would not offend against the statute or the covenant, whatever the intention or the effect. If the 1972 Act had wanted to bind the way in which buyers from a Council could act, it would have said so; but it did not. It was silent. One could not read too much into silence.

So there it was. After our hopes had been raised, it was decided that Westminster had not acted wrongly, unfairly, or unlawfully. They could sell or lease the land and, as the bench said, 'Really the point is a narrow one; it admits of no further elaboration'.

He added a rider, which was nice of him, that, as Leicester Square was one of London's ornaments, he hoped it would continue to remain so – a consoling comment.

The result was that Mr Albert Grant's covenant was still in place, but so was the great substation, under the ground. The Electricity Board decided their statutory duty to provide a supply of electricity was more important than the limiting effect of the covenant, and went ahead with their project, whatever the consequences.

The case illustrated the uncertainty of going to law. It also indicated the calm consideration given to the issues by all concerned. The judicial review process, although affording us no remedy in Leicester Square, continues to expand, setting and enforcing limits to the unacceptable face and exercise of authority. It is a fast developing area, evidence that the law itself is still running, or at least jogging.

The association and its dedicated members therefore had to suffer the lorries, the loss of business, residual doubts as to long-term effects, but they had fought a civilised battle in a civilised, responsible way.

Since the hearing of the case and the completion of the works, I have often walked around the Square. It has, to my mind, worked out better than the association members had feared, yet I am sure their action had put all concerned on their mettle.

I have a sneaking suspicion, though, that association members, the redoubtable Albert Grant MP, public benefactor and covenantor, indeed the original Tulk, would not be too displeased at the final result of the Council's efforts. Leicester Square remains the popular centre it ever was, and, as judge, association, and I all agree and hope, will never cease so to be.

Chapter XXI

Life is a Lottery

or *A Unique Campaign*

Introduction

In 1990, Mr Denis Vaughan breezed into my office. A musician of note, orchestral conductor, author, he was concerned that the arts in Britain were desperately short of funds. He compared the proliferation of opera houses and orchestras in continental Europe with the limited number in Britain. He concluded that, just as the Sydney Opera House (he stems from Australia) arose on the proceeds of a lottery, so could a national lottery in Britain enormously benefit the arts, and not only arts, but also sport and the environment.

Would I help on the legal side and also in the campaign, he enquired. He radiated enthusiasm and aroused my interest, although my experience in lotteries had been limited to advising local charities.

I had helped at various times, however, in previous public campaigns; to alter welfare laws for members of the armed forces posted overseas; for parents claiming compensation following permanent disability to children after whooping cough inoculation; for the removal of the loitering with intent (sus) provisions in the old 1824 Vagrancy Act; for a separate law to govern credit unions. I was fascinated at the way public, parliamentary, and executive opinion could be influenced by intense campaigns, often leading to a change in the law. National newspapers conduct such campaigns as a matter of course.

We discussed further. There had been lotteries in Britain since Tudor times. The year 1569 saw the first lottery in England, to fund the repair of the Cinque Ports. In 1739, a lottery produced funds for building Westminster Bridge. The British Museum was built with the proceeds of a lottery. In Europe, only two countries were then without a national lottery: the United Kingdom and Albania. An unexpected combination, and soon Albania, climbing out of communist dogmatism, fell into step with the rest of the continent of Europe, leaving Britain isolated as the sole non-lottery country. Worldwide, 170 major national and state lotteries existed in 130 countries.

Denis believed the time was ripe for a change. Having conducted musicians, he was confident he could lead an assorted collection of individuals in a performance of a new work. Certainly he looked the part. Tall, erect, athletic (a fast walker, as I later discovered), distinguished in appearance, fluent and accomplished in languages, experienced in the ways of different countries in which he had lived, he seemed suitably qualified for the arduous task of initiating and sustaining a campaign he hoped would transform much in Britain for the better.

All he needed was a structure, an organisation, an office, assistants, a group of prominent and supportive figures, access to government at all levels, public relations expertise, press and media access, and a good case. Not much to ask. At the time he possessed only one of these requirements – a good case – apart from honourable intentions, and an effervescent belief in the cause.

As time went on, the other requirements materialised, but money was a perpetual problem. It miraculously appeared at intervals, especially when a premature end to the campaign seemed inevitable due to its absence. Occasionally, the generous nature of one of its supporters bridged the gap. I had no doubt Denis and the campaign's bank manager had a number of sleepless nights; mainly the former.

I had seen dogged persistence in action before. I recognised the intensity and dedication of an individual dominated by a single-minded fervent belief. I recall a sea captain determined to buy a small, old cargo boat and sail it across the Atlantic. I advised on legalities, and the safety regulations the vessel had to satisfy to obtain the licensing authority's approval.

With a list of regulations in hand, he and I clambered over the ship, from bow to stern, port to starboard, bridge practically to hull. I never believed he would make it. I would have hesitated to take it on the Serpentine, in London's Hyde Park. When, finally, he set sail from London, I prayed for him. When I heard he had pulled in at Falmouth, I still prayed for him, hoping he would return by rail. But you can't stop such a person.

When news came that he was out in the Atlantic, proceeding due west, I hoped he was also praying. Yet months later I had the pleasure of clambering aboard the vessel as it lay securely in a Caribbean carenage. Never give up, never despair. The power of intense mental determination and belief, its effect on the physical, should never be underestimated.

The lottery campaign had one great advantage over the sea captain's mission – it was all conducted on land. It was far more involved, however, faced totally different elements, was tossed and turned by greater gusts of fortune and public policy, and reached a somewhat different haven from the one originally intended. Yet it got there in the end.

The resolution of Denis Vaughan was the central factor. For the next few years he lived the lottery daily; probably dreamed about it. One day, I have little doubt, he will compose a lottery symphony or concerto, probably in A flat or B major.

A lawyer is usually an onlooker in cases of this type, creating a legal structure and watching legal points along the way. I found myself, however, also a campaigner, albeit on a modest scale. By dint of enormous effort and with great flair Denis achieved his objective. The National Lottery emerged and developed, not quite as he had envisaged, but in a controlled, balanced and beneficial form. A vast public debt is due to a premier performance of no mean quality by Denis Vaughan, accompanied and supported by a rare collection of leading players on the national scene.

The Story

On 25th January 1993, Mr Peter Brooke, Secretary of State for National Heritage, rose in the House of Commons. He begged to move 'that the bill be now read a second time'. Thus came the National Lottery Bill before MPs, with full government backing. Yet behind that simple phrase lay three years of intense campaigning.

Denis Vaughan and I had discussed a structure for the campaign. We registered a private liability company limited by guarantee; no shareholders, only directors. Although some of the objects had overtones accepted as charitable – the arts, culture, the environment – the means were political, and so no registration with the Charity Commissioners was possible. The organisation was called The Lottery Promotion Company Limited, an exact description of its function. It then began to promote.

The first need was to acquire directors of distinction. This was to be a national campaign leading to what Peter Brooke later described as 'establishing a major new industry', a vision 'which will improve the quality of life of the citizens of this country'.

By 1990, fervour for care of the environment had reached its peak. Every prime minister was convening conferences. Climate change and the greenhouse effect were in the air. Hence provision of funds to preserve and enhance the environment – a lottery objective – aroused widespread interest and support.

The arts, as ever, needed money. The Arts Council, and its supporting minister, had an annual tussle with the mandarins of the Treasury over funding. With the lottery in existence, a tremendous boost to the arts was anticipated. Arts included museums. Early on in the campaign a national museum rang me, innocently asking for funds. I could not oblige.

The third main objective was the furtherance of sport. Sports Councils had ambitions that could not be fulfilled. Britain's relatively poor showing in the Olympic Games was partially attributed to the lack of facilities. Indeed, as Sir Ivan Lawrence, who had introduced a private lottery bill in the House of Commons less than six months earlier, stated:

'We will be able to spend more on covered tennis courts, athletic tracks, and sports halls. France has 20 times as many tennis courts, and Germany 20 times as many swimming pools, as we do. There are 50,000 swimmers in this country, but if they want Olympic-standard training they can choose from only 12 swimming pools.'

He made a further point that the more facilities there were for lively teenagers, the less likelihood was there of juvenile crime.

The opportunity was there. From nowhere but a lottery could the means come to help the environment, the arts, and sport on the scale required. Denis had a good case. He needed well-known supporters, and he found them. Whilst later David Astor, Lord Montagu and Stephen Rubin, all prominent figures, joined the Board, and urbane, cultured Sir Richard Luce participated for a period, the heat of the campaign was borne by a few remarkably dedicated men, of all political parties and none.

Lord Michael Birkett, with a notable record in arts and the theatre, perennially exuded a buoyant and infectious youthfulness. Sir Eddie Kulukundis – shipper, impresario, sports activist – gave unstintingly of his time, a man generous in heart and pocket.

Dennis Howell, later Lord Howell, former Minister of Sport (unfairly dubbed in forgotten years as the 'minister for rain'), had a directness of approach and a perception of reality as to what was and was not possible that guided his colleagues invaluably, and certainly opened my eyes to political realities.

Lord Gibson, former chairman of the National Trust, spread a calm, cautious wisdom and realism that admirably tempered airborne enthusiasms. The Earl of Harewood, elegant in appearance and expression, with a rare depth and breadth of experience, made up the board. All played their part fully, in fact as well as in name.

I enjoyed every board meeting. They were an education. I was amused at the confidential assessment of personalities, of ministers, civil servants; intrigued at plans to reach prominent power centres through intermediate agencies and individuals. We soon identified friends and foes.

Friends were varied in character. Some had long advocated the principle of a national lottery; commercial concerns hoped to obtain franchises to operate aspects of the scheme, and a vast range of recipients of lottery funds were inevitably supportive.

Ranged against the National Lottery were some strange bedfellows. Some were opposed on principle to the very idea. There was opposition from some religious groups. Interestingly, in Holland, the country with the oldest national lottery, churches had no problem, individual churches often benefiting from lotteries. There was no opposition in largely Catholic countries, but there was an understandable viewpoint of some religious leaders that a lottery was gambling and gambling was evil. One clergyman Member of Parliament in the Commons debate quoted a view he had previously expressed: 'The desire and aim to get money without doing the equivalent of necessary work strikes at the heart of the well-being of mankind.'

He was therefore opposed to the principle of gambling. It was believed Margaret Thatcher shared that view and her replacement, in 1991, by John Major as Prime Minister was an encouragement to our directors.

Most potent opposition came from the football pools promoters. For decades they had had a clear field in the gambling world, although selection of football results was still peculiarly regarded as an exercise of skill. Kenneth Baker, former Home Secretary, confirmed in the debate:

'The pools have enjoyed a privileged position for many years. In effect, three companies have had a monopoly in pool soft gambling. I am not surprised they are not welcoming competition with open arms'.

Mr Baker glowingly added, 'the bill will substantially increase the sum of human happiness'. Who could argue with that? He almost echoed the Minister's enthusiastic words of introduction when he added:

'The Bill will create a great deal of cheer around the country. The Government needs a bill to cheer people up'.

Had I realised all this when drafting the Memorandum of Association of the company I would have added a further objects clause, namely, 'To cheer up the people and increase the sum of human happiness'. The reaction of the Registrar of Companies would have been intriguing.

Throughout the campaign I had the impression the pools people, (who, after all, had a case – namely the protection of their profits), had been trying too hard. They had retained expensive consultants and public relations firms. They had even obtained, at the last minute, a tax concession in the 1991 Budget linked to creating a foundation for arts and sport. They had lobbied MPs extensively; perhaps too extensively, reflected in Mr Brooke's comment, 'The pools companies have been lobbying all who would listen'.

This strategy, I believed, was flawed, as it played on fear, on inadequate statistics, and on an overkill of representations that rebounded. They tried to equate the pools with the lottery, which was unconvincing since the aim of the pools was private profit, whilst the lottery aimed at public good.

Opposition too came from Members of Parliament representing constituencies where pools employees lived: Liverpool, Cardiff, Glasgow. It was feared 6,000 people would lose their jobs if the lottery made too large an impact on the popularity of the pools. Again, a reasonable point, one on which the official Labour Opposition divided the House.

Our response was twofold: first, that the lottery would appeal to a different market and have little effect on those who like a weekly flutter on the pools; secondly that the lottery would release funds for an enormous programme of public construction, creating 80,000 jobs or more.

But even further changes were wrought in our original proposals by an impeccable source, one we had not considered sufficiently early on. This was the great body of thousands of charities, who feared that funds usually donated to them would be diverted into the lottery. Their case was effectively put by the National Council of Voluntary Associations, and became part of the final scheme placed before Parliament. Again they had a legitimate point, but, unlike the pools, had an effective ear to the ground and an eye for the most persuasive avenues of approach to the powers-that-be.

Hovering over all our efforts were the acquisitive long arms and hands of Her Majesty's Treasury. We tried to minimise their desire to claw in as much as they could. Our initial view had been an annual lottery income of £3 billion which, after half went to prizes and a further percentage to administration, would leave about £1 billion for the three good causes; no mean sum, and a wonderful boost to the environment, arts and sport.

We soon discovered a mass of alternative figures thrown about, from accountants, policy centres, City finance houses, the European Community in Brussels. We discovered too what we believed to be major errors in Treasury estimates and forecasts, particularly as to the total spent annually on gambling in Britain.

Our figures, it later appeared, were closer to reality than either the Treasury's or the accountants. This experience left me suspicious of any future Treasury forecasts on anything, seemingly confirmed later by changes within the Treasury advisory structure. The Treasury wanted its cut, its pound of lottery flesh, to compensate, as it saw it, for anticipated loss of public revenue elsewhere.

These then were the forces that, for three years, hoped either to defeat or amend the proposals of the Lottery Promotion Company. The way the battle was fought, the campaign conducted by the directors, was exemplary. There was energy, honesty, clarity. They relied on facts, the spread of true information, the rebuttal of mis-information. There was daily attention to the press, to all the media, to Parliament, Government, civil servants. The cause was canvassed at party conferences. Leaders of overseas national and state lotteries addressed specially-convened meetings. It was a notable and remarkable campaign, conducted on a shoestring, constantly contending with the understandable fears that change always engenders.

How often do I recall sitting with Denis, drafting and re-drafting press releases and letters to ministers, responding to inaccuracies in the media, finally joining the directors in a visit to the Minister in his sumptuous National Heritage Ministry, with its vast spaces and strange paintings, learning of the proposals shortly to be placed before Parliament.

We had not got the plan we had when we began. There remained many battles ahead, but we had succeeded in getting the principle of a national lottery established. Environment became heritage, and to this, together with sports and art, were added charities and an entirely new idea – a Millenium Fund to celebrate the survival of the nation to the year 2000. So five objectives replaced three, the heritage item being of an embracing nature, encompassing, as the Minister put it, 'the natural as well as the built heritage'.

Thus The National Lottery Bill, with its 56 clauses, 10 schedules, 45 closely-worded pages, was launched onto the Parliamentary sea. One felt like saying, after such an intensive period of preparation, 'God bless her and all who sail in her'.

Denis and colleagues had fought a prolonged and difficult campaign. I had been fascinated by its progress. It showed what could be achieved in an open democracy by the sustained effort of a band of gifted, perceptive, and dedicated men in a campaign which has already had a major effect on the well-being and facilities of the land and its people. As hundreds of millions of pounds are allotted to so many worthy causes, I hope the recipients, as well as prize-winners, recognise the debt they owe to Denis Vaughan, the man who never gave up, and who is the real founder of Britain's National Lottery.

Chapter XXII

Nowt So Queer As Folk
or *A Brief Glance at the Human Race*

As I write, cases and faces crowd in on my brain. Some I have described, many others remain unrecorded. What fascinates me so enormously, in ecological terms, is the bio-diversity of our species, not merely physically, but mentally, emotionally, spiritually. I could, without difficulty, catalogue a lengthy list of virtues and vices, illustrating each one by a case, a face, an issue, an expression, a brief, but memorable encounter.

I have seen generosity in action. Arriving at my office one morning I found a massive bulk encased in reams of cardboard as tall as myself. What on earth could it be? On investigation I found myself to be the new owner of two magnificent hardwood carvings of Ashanti kings and their musicians. Grateful clients from Ghana had despatched, at no inconsiderable cost to themselves, this weighty but precious gift. Bottles of most acceptable and stimulating rum appeared regularly from all parts of the Caribbean, as well as shining reproductions of exotic temples from India.

I have seen, too, dignity, self-respect and humility in action. Often those who achieve high office or great wealth acquire habits of arrogance. How heart-warming it is to find men and women of eminence unaffected by the temptations of power. I recall the naturalness and simple humanity of Dame Nita Barrow, the calm practicality of Dame Cicely Saunders, founder of the hospice movement, the immense learning, worn lightly and humbly, of diplomat and human rights leader, Dr. L.M. Singhvi.

I once had the privilege of introducing our present Queen Elizabeth individually to some delegates at a Commonwealth Conference, and rarely have I seen such a combination of charm, lack of affectation, and sense of duty, as she displayed on that occasion.

These were not clients but people I had had the rare opportunity of meeting in the course of my daily and communal work.

As I write, in September 1997, the world mourns the death of Princess Diana and Mother Teresa, celebrated people who gave of themselves, people who cared deeply. And yet, among my clients, I have often seen caring and self-sacrifice of a like nature, unreported, unsung, unhonoured. I recall the eleven-year-old child, cherished by her parents, who was seriously and permanently injured in a road accident. From that moment on, those parents gave of themselves without hesitation, year in, year out, to help their afflicted daughter. I have seen self-sacrifice, love in action.

Not unnaturally, this spirit of caring concern has been evidenced in many of the nurses and doctors I have represented. I was so struck by the love shown by the matron of a famous maternity hospital whom I had helped over the years, that I readily agreed, in response to her request, to become the hospital's Father Christmas. I only hope my peregrinations around the wards, bedecked in red cloak and hood, flowing white beard and moustache, distributing gifts, amused, rather than alarmed, the reclining patients.

One doctor, quite eminent, yet a man of humility, I represented for years. Those two qualities do not always go together in the profession. I once questioned him in a Coroners Court. I asked, 'what was the cause of the deceased's death?' 'Because he did not want to live', replied the learned doctor, ignoring the ostensible cause inscribed in medical terms on the death certificate. Such a response is rare in a profession as much addicted to jargon as my own.

I have seen, too, consuming selfishness in action, arrogance, dogmatism, a wife forced to endure the unendurable for the sake of her children, because of a cruel husband's treatment, a husband deserted by a woman overflowing with egoism, who abandoned her young children, leaving the man to be father and mother to them.

Dogmatism in religion has afflicted both private and public affairs. I have seen this result in hypocrisy of the lowest kind, the ostentatious mouthing of prayers and elevated moral sentiments, whilst at the same time living a life of lies, deceit and greed. If anything roused me to exclaim, 'O! ye vipers and hypocrites', it was this chasm between public profession of virtue and private display of heartlessness.

On a lighter note, I recall being asked to administer an oath to a committee of Humanists. I took along with me a variety of holy books on which they could swear to the truth of the documents they were signing, but, being honest men and women, they declined all forms of holy writ and oath-taking and simply affirmed. No God, but no hypocrisy.

I recall too a dogmatic atheist holding forth loudly and disturbingly at a dinner given by clients. 'There are no absolute values, no absolute truths', he assured us, 'there is nothing absolute. Everything is relative.' He was quite positive in his view and could not be moved by argument from the assembled diners. 'Are you absolutely sure?' I asked quietly. He subsided into silence amidst the general ensuing hilarity. O! the dogmatic rigid mind! How often have I seen it, and how much misery it has caused.

And O! the sheer variety of people, their attitudes and achievements. I recall the former Israeli army oficer who, unbelievably, thought in Latin, the maggot-breeder who exuded the smell of his profession whenever arriving in the office, the Olympic weight-lifting champion, downcast by an air charter failure, a great hulk of a man, sitting in my office, head in hands, weeping profusely.

I recall dancing through the streets of Port-of-Spain during Trinidad Carnival at the invitation of a former mayor of that city – incredible rhythm and enthusiasm. A further strange experience deriving from my work was acting as judge in a major beauty competition. No hardship this. At the other end of the spectrum was a World Immunological Conference to which I became the legal adviser. What was I doing among all those earnest experts mouthing incomprehensible words?

Then there was the reception given for me in Washington DC in 1995 by the local body of judges in the Court House. A great honour, but also an opportunity to study the variety of backgrounds from which these judicial dignitaries had emerged,

I pondered too about those wealthy people who had asked me to set up trusts for their children and who then bewailed the disintegration of those children, emerging into adulthood, spoiled by wealth for which they had not striven, and which had weakened their moral, and often physical, fibre.

My mind goes back to the jovial secondary school headteacher who ran a bar in his school after the children had left. He had the most successful parents association in the borough.

So many experiences, so many faces, so many examples of the unbelievable variety of human attributes and patterns of behaviour.

I found that the experience of years had developed in me antennae that operated as a natural lie-detector. Colleagues can testify to their own growth of the same bump of perception. There is the sense of shame and guilt that afflicts some, often needlessly. This emerged frequently in family problems. The client set out a story, perhaps a basis for divorce, which I instinctively knew was but a superficial recital, whilst the real story was embedded deep down in words undeclared.

It required patience, and time, to get to the true heart of a problem, probing and gently questioning, removing slowly layers of guilt-ridden shame. How often was the ultimate reality based on physical and sexual issues, now the stock-in-trade of the lower media, publicly trumpeted, but in former times, matters of intimate delicacy and private silence. So often an interview took on the character of a confessional as one learned of the wide range of sexual proclivities of our remarkable species.

Courage, too, I have seen, the courage of the Holocaust survivors who asked me to help them, the simple courage of those who stood up fearlessly for the cause of basic human rights, whether in totalitarian communist states or African dictatorships. Other clients, men of distinction, sought my help in obtaining asylum in Britain whilst concerned daily that the long arm of Middle Eastern terrorism should not reach them here in London.

What a race of beings we are, slowly, painfully, evolving, full of contradictions, so different in our thoughts, values and beliefs, one from another, yet still having so much in common, perhaps a source of future human unity. My career has brought me face to face with all these human qualities, all these human deficiencies. I say 'face to face' though I rarely sat across a desk from a client. I usually sat next to the person who consulted me, beside him or her, informally, without tension, with no legal 'iron curtain' of a large and prestigious desk to separate us. It was more human that way, more normal, more natural.

I recall so many cases, many faces, many encounters, much sadness, yet also much joy and good humour. I am grateful to all those clients, many of whom have remained personal friends. They gave me an insight into our strange breed, and enriched me with a stream of endless experiences, a constant source of challenge, of fascination, and of wonder.

Chapter XXIII

Of the Nature of Things

The practice of the law, as I hope I have been able to suggest, is demanding, fascinating, intensely practical. Feet have to remain firmly on the ground. I would be happy to explain the technicalities of commercial transactions in which I have been involved, but they revolve around money, and I (and hopefully you) am more interested in people than in dollars and pounds sterling, though the latter are crucial to daily living. Man does not live by bread alone, provided he has bread. Yet, at times, it is useful to sit back and look at the deeper level below the one on which a lawyer operates daily.

For example, when dealing with abortion cases, I rarely thought about the more fundamental question of the nature of the particular life that was created, then terminated before living out his or her allotted span, or indeed the nature of life itself.

Similarly, what is the significance of a husband helping to end the suffering of his incurably ill wife? That arose in the case of a prominent journalist. I used to see him and the wife and advise on their legal affairs. What should my attitude have been had I known that he had been instrumental in ending her life, at her request, even though out of compassion? He later went on to become an enthusiastic campaigner for euthanasia. The thought arises: Do we have the right to say who will live and who will die?

The issue was widely discussed on television, and the programmes were seen by our 21-year-old son, who at the time lay dying from cancer. Despite his own severe pain and remote chance of recovery, he told my wife and me that he was resolutely opposed to euthanasia. He did not think anyone was entitled to take the life of another. The story of his steadiness in adversity, his quiet courage, allied to his remarkable creativity, I have recorded fully in another book as a tribute to the quality of his life, and as an acknowledgment of his constant inspiration to us.

I recall the occasion when a talented young woman died suddenly. The signs were that, in a fit of depression, she had taken her own life. Her family were anxious that the coroner's jury should not bring in a verdict of suicide. I managed to persuade them accordingly. The family could not bear to think the deceased had rejected them, and life itself. Suicide is not merely a rejection of oneself, or of life, or even of religious teaching, but also of all those who have been close to the suicide, and who have to live with memories, so often with anguish.

In murder cases we were so concerned with the nature of the evidence, whether the charge could be reduced to manslaughter, the technical and evidential battles, the whole accusatorial, gladiatorial system, that we forgot about the non-legal, non-lawyer's aspect of the cases, involving, deliberately or accidentally, the destruction of a human life; destruction thereby of a whole world. What did that mean in the wider scheme of things? Such thoughts rarely crossed our minds.

I think back particularly over the abortion cases. In my earliest years in the profession I was involved in a major case at the Old Bailey, where two doctors were tried for illegally performing abortions, before the Abortion Act had reached the statute book. A parade of women, from duchesses to students, described in detail in the witness box how they became pregnant; how scared they were of disclosing the news to husbands, fathers, family, friends; how they had resorted to the two doctors, who had helped them expertly, not primarily for money, but out of their understanding of the effect of unwanted pregnancies on all concerned.

In a similar case some some years later,; a doctor and a nurse helped young women out of situations where the pregnancies, if allowed to continue, would have fundamentally affected the future lives of the women concerned.

Again the accused helped the girls, not for money, but out of social convictions. That was one view of abortion. Opponents of that view would claim that, in every case, defenceless human life which had come into existence had been murdered. We practitioners of the law never thought about these aspects of life. We were too busy defending the accused. We rarely looked deeper than the level of the law, and the case in hand.

The abortion debate continues with heated confrontation, particularly in the United States, posed as a right to life on the one hand, and a right of a woman's sovereignty over her own body on the other – a proposition I am not sure is correctly formulated.

Can the former say, with any certainty, at what stage the spirit enters the growing embryo and foetus, so that one is destroying a life?

In all these cases – murder, euthanasia, suicide, abortion – the issue is the sanctity of human life. Many religions speak of these things and have established moral guidelines which legal systems try to reflect. The more moral a society, the less need is there for the criminal law: the more violent and immoral a society, the more are laws and courts necessary.

Certainly most religions teach of the prolongation of life beyond our human frame, and thereby vastly widen our perspective. Most religions also teach a high level of morality. That is the acceptable face of religion.

At the same time, those same religions, in practice and in their organised forms, have shown scant regard for the sanctity of human life, have justified the destruction of life, have called each other infidels, devils, enemies of the true God and the true faith, and, in the name of each particular God, have slaughtered each other indiscriminately. We are still no more than moral and religious adolescents, whatever our resplendent titles, garments and rituals; however sophisticated our religious and secular laws.

Over the years I have advised religious bodies of various faiths, guided some through legal quagmires, helped them to comply with charity laws, established constitutions and legal structures through which they could breathe their dedicated messages.

Perhaps one of the most intriguing set of clients have been the psychics. With few exceptions, they would not claim to be people of intellectual pretensions, but they gave yet another perspective on the meaning of life and of the nature of things.

I recall the world-famous direct voice medium, Leslie Flint, who became not only a client but a close friend. I advised a spiritualist church in a few of its practical problems. For a time I helped the prestigious College of Psychic Studies, founded in the 19th century, and adorned in its leadership by figures such as Sir Arthur Conan Doyle, the noted scientist Sir Oliver Lodge, and Rosamund Lehmann, celebrated novelist and author.

I was even invited to lecture to the college, and was surprised to see that the audience consisted not of elderly people on the fringe of the social scene, but bank managers, professors, members of the main professions, and particularly a large number of young men and women in their twenties and thirties.

The books of the college library and the messages recorded over 50 years of Leslie Flint's mediumship, both extensive and wide-ranging, contain teachings and ideas that gave an even broader dimension to our understanding of the nature of things.

Life is eternal. Experiences in one or more lives on this planet are necessary for individual development. Neither murder, abortion, nor suicide do in fact terminate life, though they affect spiritual progress. Pain and suffering are as endemic to the human condition as are love and joy. Thoughts are alive and real, conditioning everything. A single human life, pulled up and down by a higher and lower inheritance, is merely a spiritual being expressed in physical terms.

The consequences of these ideas, if reflected in public and private life, are enormous. They could revolutionise human society; could substitute new laws, universal laws, for our present legislation; could create turmoil in all established religious organisations, though not among truly religious individuals (always a small minority); could affect the racial and ethnic views groups hold of themselves and of others; could, in effect, make demands far above the capacity of the overwhelming majority of people to respond, and are therefore in no danger of being put into effect, even though, without some positive movement in their direction, our human species may continue to destroy itself and its habitat.

Speculation as to the nature of things is a luxury I can afford at the time of writing. It is not something on which daily practitioners of the law can afford to spend time. The morning post, the urgent telephone call, the even more urgent fax message and more lately e-mail, internet, and heaven knows what next, court and procedural deadlines and appearances, the drafting of documents, interviews with clients and witnesses, negotiating of personal injury and other claims, the demands of a phalanx of registries, probate, divorce, companies, trade marks, the equally urgent submissions to a parade of tribunals – financial, industrial, immigration, social security – all these and much more are the daily stock in trade and dominant activity of the busy lawyer.

They are the nature of his or her things. They may touch on wider, deeper issues, but there is little time to ponder on universal themes.

There are law journals to read, law reports to study, seminars to support, committees to attend. These are reality enough, and one reality at a time is more than enough to manage for the woman and the man of law.

And yet the lawyer, the non-commercial lawyer especially, deals daily with the very stuff of human life: human emotions, human relationships, indeed human freedom. It is important he or she should know the law, understand the fine art which is the practice of the law. It is also important that, at times, the lawyer should sit quietly and catch a glimpse of a greater reality of which his or her world is but a small and temporary part, and understand that there exist laws more profound and more lasting than those which are his or her daily concern.